Playing GRANDMA'S Games

By Karen South Arnold

WESTERN REFLECTIONS PUBLISHING COMPANY

Ouray, CO

First Edition
Printed in the United States of America

ISBN 1-890437-47-6
Library of Congress Catalog Number 00-102411
Cover and text design by Laurie Goralka Design

Western Reflections Publishing Company
P.O. Box 710
Ouray, CO 81427

To my parents, Maxine H. and George P. South,
who opened my eyes to games,

To Ellery W. Heiss, my grandfather,
who always beat me at cribbage,

And to Bill Cunningham,
who entices my child out to play.

Thank you, one and all.

Karen South Arnold
Montrose, CO
March 2000

FOREWORD

Games are one of the few activities that transcend cultural, linguistic, geographic, social, and political differences in peoples around the globe. It may be that games are inherent to man's psychological makeup: authors throughout history have mentioned that characteristic. For example, Alfonso X (The Learned), king of Leon and Castille, personally supervised a series of books on history, law, religion, astronomy, magic, and games. His *Libro de Juegos* (Book of Games) attests to their importance in medieval life. Publishing in 1283, he wrote, "God has intended men to enjoy themselves with many games." In 1938, Johan Huizinga published his treatise Homo Ludens (Man, the Games Player). In it he states, "genuine, pure play is one of the main bases of civilization."

The purpose of this book is to introduce the reader to a wide variety of games that were played in America from the beginning of European immigration into the nineteenth century. We were a game-playing bunch in our formative years!

It was difficult to choose which games to include (and exclude) in this book. Initially I opted to exclude historic games that are still popular and readily available (e.g., backgammon, parcheesi). I also omitted those that have complex systems or rules and a surplus of instructional materials (e.g., chess, bridge). I included in each section at least one game that seemed quintessential (e.g., draughts, the game of goose, hopscotch) — games that were immensely popular and fathered many variations. Other criteria for inclusion were a variety in the number of players and location (inside and outside) and equipment that was minimal or easy to obtain or make. Finally, I added a few of my own favorites. Perhaps they will become some of your favorites as well. . . .

MAKING GAME EQUIPMENT

Most of the equipment used in these games you can make yourself. One common item was the teetotem. It is a six-sided top, the sides of which have numbers or dots from 1 to 6. When the teetotem is spun between the fingers, the side landing down determines the number of spaces a player can move. A simple teetotem can be made by gluing a hexagon with numbers or dots to a piece of cardboard and pushing a sharpened pencil through the center. You can carve your own teetotem from a piece of wood. Or you can make a number disc with a spinning metal arrow fastened into the cardboard with a brad.

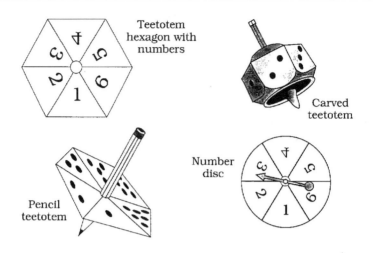

Teetotem hexagon with numbers

Carved teetotem

Pencil teetotem

Number disc

Playing pieces for board games are limited only by your imagination. They can be as simple as distinctive buttons or rocks, or you can fashion something into elaborate objects. Expecially in the Indian games chapter, a number of ideas are given for making playing pieces from natural objects.

Most of the boards in this book are based on elegant earlier concepts. They have been simplified to accommodate space and computer art. If you want to reproduce and enlarge them to make a better playing surface, that's perfectly okay. Some replicas of old board games, such as the game of goose, are available from suppliers. The books listed in the bibliography have great models: those by Arnold and Goodfellow show pictures of ornate game boards and tables, those by the Provenzos and Grunfeld have diagrams and construction plans.

A few of the game boards and other playing materials, such as lacrosse rackets and the shove-groat board, are a little more complicated to make, but the instructions are detailed enough to allow you to tackle those projects successfully.

CONVENTIONS USED IN THIS BOOK

Classification of the games into the chapters is somewhat arbitrary. Most games, especially card and Indian games, lend themselves to wagering on the outcome (e.g., farkle, bell and hammer, pope joan). Others, such as quoits and draughts, are enjoyed by both children and adults alike.

Cards are portrayed in their modern configurations; that is, they are double-ended and have numbers in the corners. The goal is to have you start playing the games easily. If you want to use period-appropriate cards, they can be obtained from the suppliers in the back of the book.

Card games in this book are described with the following conventions:

1. Unless numbers are relevant, cards below court cards are identified as "x." An ace is A; a king, K; a queen, Q; and a jack, J.
2. Suits are identified as: clubs, ♣; diamonds, ♦; hearts, ♥; spades, ♠.
3. Selecting partners and seating, choosing the dealer, and other conventions not directly related to the play of the game are omitted.
4. Penalties for misdeals, misplays, etc., are not discussed unless they affect scoring. Standard card texts, such as Hoyle, give those rules if you want to know them.

The Indian games are primarily extrapolated from Culin's book, *Games of the North American Indians*. His anthropological data regarding scorekeeping is game-specific and often complex. Scholars of Native American culture now know that scorekeeping systems were very fluid. With that in mind, and to emphasize *playing* the games, I have suggested substitute scorekeeping methods if the original systems were elaborate.

CONTENTS

Games
for
Adults

GAMES FOR ADULTS

Games are as old as mankind itself; they have helped define the lifestyle of even the most primitive peoples. Surviving records, paintings, and artifacts show games similar to those of today being played in ancient times.

But games also adapt to reflect changing culture and values. In the Age of Enlightenment (eighteenth and nineteenth centuries), the growth in trades and exploration contributed to a dramatic increase in the middle class. Education became critical to participation in the new wealth. One aim of games was to set one's self against others and win – preparation by example for competition in a working world. The proliferation of board games reflected the social life and new geographical discoveries, strategic maneuvers of war (chess, draughts, nine men's morris), politics, and the hunt with uneven opponents (fox and geese). One has only to look at the artistry of rococo game boards – their fanciful, excessive intricacy and ornamentation – to understand how games can reflect a current cultural milieu.

DRAUGHTS (CHECKERS)

Its origins are vague, but perhaps draughts began in France as early as the twelfth century, borrowing the board from chess, the pieces from backgammon, and the moves from alquerque. Capture of pieces was optional until the sixteenth century; with compulsory capture, new versions proliferated. The game moved to England and on to the United States, where it was renamed checkers. The French voyageurs in the 1700s were avid draughts players.

There are many old draughts games: Polish, Spanish, Turkish, German, Italian, and even a losing draughts! The rules, layout, and playing board of all these games vary somewhat, but all retain the flavor of early draughts.

Object of the game. To capture all opponent's men or block them so they are unable to move.

Number of players. Two.

Terms.
"Capturing": Jumping over an opponent's piece diagonally to a vacant square on the other side of it and removing it from the board

"Crowning": Making a king by placing another playing piece on top of a piece that has reached the back row of the opponent

Equipment. A playing board with sixty-four squares, alternating dark and light. Traditional play is on the dark squares and the board is aligned so a light square is at the bottom right-hand corner for each player. Each player has twelve playing pieces that, to start, are arranged on the board as shown.

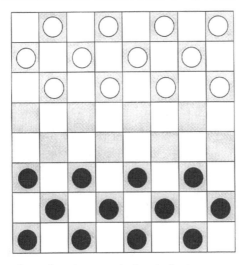

Playing draughts. The player with the dark pieces moves first. Each player moves only one piece per turn. A piece can move forward one diagonal square or capture an opponent's piece.

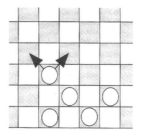

Moving one space forward diagonally

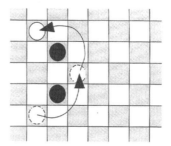

Jumping opponent's pieces to a vacant diagonal square

If multiple captures are possible in a player's single turn, they must be made, but each opponent's piece may be jumped only once. If a player fails to make a capture or to complete a series of possible captures, his opponent has three choices:

He may insist the correct moves be made and the piece moved in error be returned to its previous position

He may allow the incorrect move to stand if it is in his favor, or

He may remove from the board the piece that should have made the possible capture. This does not count as a turn, so he then continues his own turn

If two or more routes for capture(s) are possible during a player's turn, he may choose which to make. He does not have to make the move resulting in the most captures, but he must make all possible captures with the piece he chooses.

When a piece reaches the back row of the opposing side, the piece becomes a king, identified by stacking another piece of the same color on top. At the back row, that turn ends, even if more captures are possible. A king may move both backward or forward, either one square at a time or during capturing. A king may be captured by another king or a single piece.

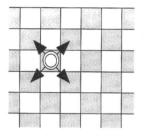

King moving one space
diagonally, either forward
or backward

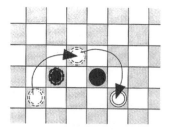

Jumping opponent's pieces to a
vacant diagonal square, either
forward or backward

The game is won by the player who removes all his opponent's pieces or blocks them so that no further moves may be made.

SOME VARIATIONS OF DRAUGHTS

Loser draughts. In this variation, players try to lose their pieces or position them so they cannot move. The playing board, playing pieces, and rules are basically the same as draughts. Instead of the player's piece being removed from the board when a player fails to capture an opponent's piece, however, the opponent requests that the player make the capture. Moreover, if there are several possible jumps, the opponent requests that the move be made that captures the most pieces — the object is to lose pieces!

Continental (Polish) draughts. Continental (Polish) draughts was first played in Paris in the 1720s. The game is played on a one hundred-square board with each player having twenty pieces. Another major difference is the versatility in moving queens (instead of kings).

Each player puts his pieces on the board in the starting position.

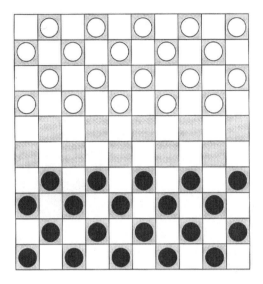

Each piece normally moves diagonally forward one square. When jumping to capture, however, a piece may jump diagonally forward *and/or* backward.

If a player has a choice of one capture or more than one capture, he must make the multiple capture. If the quantity of two possible captures is equal, the one that does the most damage (e.g., capturing a queen) must be made. An opponent's piece may never be jumped more than once within a capturing move.

A piece is crowned queen when it gets to the opponent's back row at the end of a turn. If a piece gets to the back row but must move out to continue capturing, it does not become a queen until it lands there finally at the end of another turn.

A queen has the power to move diagonally any number of vacant squares in one move.

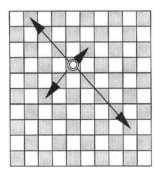

A queen also may land on any diagonally vacant square after capturing a piece.

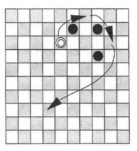

The game ends when one player has taken all of his opponent's pieces or blocked any subsequent moves.

Diagonal draughts. This variation is played with the same board and rules as draughts, but the playing pieces are positioned on diagonally opposite corners of the board. If the board is placed with a dark square at the lower right for each player, each uses nine playing pieces and there are three squares on each corner for making kings (marked with K below). The board can also be oriented so a light square is at the bottom right; then there are four squares on the corners for achieving a king (K) and each player begins with twelve playing pieces.

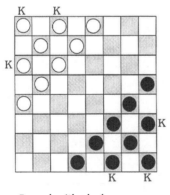

Board with dark square on lower right

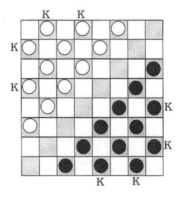

Board with light square on lower right

CHIVALRY

Chivalry, one of many battle games produced by Parker Brothers during the late 1800s, was described in the company's catalogue as the best board game to come along in 2,000 years.

Object of the game. To be the first player to place two pieces in the stronghold spaces on the opponent's side of the board.

Number of players. Two.

Terms.
"Cantoring": Jumping over a player's own piece — horizontally, vertically, or diagonally — into the vacant square on the opposite side. A player may jump as many of his own pieces as possible within one turn, but does not have to cantor, even if such a move is possible

"Jumping": Jumping an opponent's piece — horizontally, vertically, or diagonally — into the vacant contiguous square. A player must make a jump move whenever it is possible and continue to jump all pieces available within the same turn. The opponent's jumped piece(s) are removed from the board

Equipment. A playing board with 176 squares. The stronghold squares are marked with stars on opposite sides of the board. Each player has twenty pieces of a distinctive color — twelve are pawns and eight are knights.

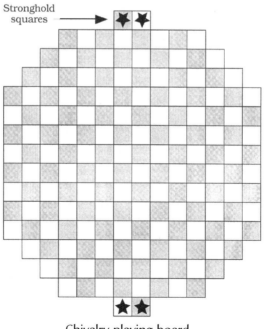

Chivalry playing board

Playing chivalry. Each player places his pieces on the board as shown. They decide who will take the first turn.

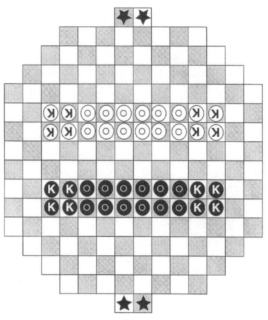

Both pawns and knights can move three different ways:

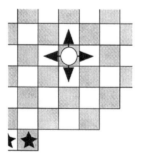

Moving one space vertically or horizontally, but not diagonally

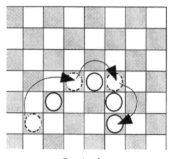

Cantoring

Jumping

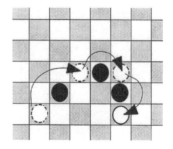

Depending on whether the piece is a pawn or a knight, however, restrictions apply in combining moves:

Pawns can move one space, cantor, or jump, but cannot combine any of the three types of moves in any one turn.

Knights may never combine advancing one space with a cantor or jump. They can combine cantoring with jumping opponent's pieces, but all cantors must precede any jumps.

The game is won when one player places a piece in each of his opponent's two stronghold spaces on the opposite side of the board.

GO-BANG

Go-bang is believed to have been invented in China over 3,000 years ago. This game of strategy became popular in America during the nineteenth century. It was often played on a folded slate which could be carried in players' pockets.

Object of the game. To be the first player to form a straight line of five pieces — horizontally, vertically, or diagonally.

Number of players. Two.

Equipment. The traditional game is a board with eighteen squares marked off in each direction. Playing pieces are aligned on the intersecting lines.

A later version is played on a board of one hundred squares, ten horizontally and ten vertically. With this board, the pieces are aligned in the squares.

With either board, each player also has a set of fifty distinctively colored playing pieces.

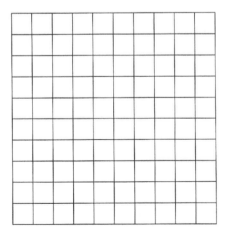

100-square go-bang playing board

Playing go-bang. Players select their pieces; the one with the darker pieces plays first. Players alternate turns, placing one piece anywhere on the board. Once a piece is placed, it cannot be moved until the game is over.

A player wins when he succeeds in placing five pieces in a row before his opponent can do so. The game ends in a tie if neither player forms a five-piece row before all pieces are placed on the board.

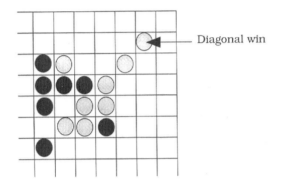

Diagonal win

QUEEN'S GUARD

Queen's guard combines the strategic complexity of chess with the simple moves of checkers. It was very popular during the Victorian Era.

Objective. To be the first player to position the queen in the central space on the board and surround her with the six guard pieces.

Number of players. Two.

Equipment. A hexagonal playing board of ninety-one smaller hexagons. Each player has seven pieces distinctive from those of his opponent; one of the seven is the queen, the other six pieces are guards.

Playing queen's guard. Each player puts his pieces on the board in one of two different ways. In the first, the queens are placed in opposite corners with the guards in alternating positions around the edge of the board. In the second, the players take turns placing their pieces wherever they choose on the outer edge.

Pieces are moved one space forward or sideways. Once a piece has been moved toward the center of the board, it cannot be moved back toward the outer edge. If a player touches a piece, he must move that piece or lose his turn.

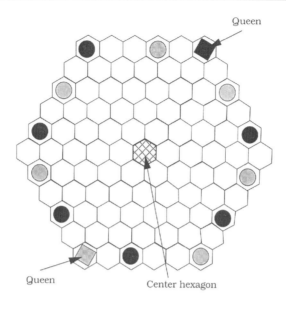

Queen's Guard Board with Queens
in Opposite Corners

If a guard is flanked between an opponent's pieces (ignoring possible moves), the player must move it to any vacant space on the outer edge of the board in his next turn. If a queen is flanked, the player must move her to any vacant space chosen by his opponent for his next turn.

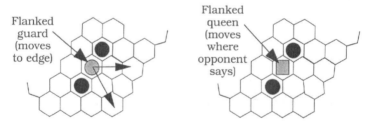

If a player has more than one piece flanked when it becomes his turn, he must continue to use his turns until all of his flanked pieces are returned

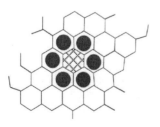

to the outer edge (or, for queens, where the opponent dictates). Guards may be returned in any order, but if a queen is one of the flanked pieces, she must be moved first.

Only the queen can be moved to the central hexagon. A player forfeits the game if he encloses an empty central hexagon with his guards.

The first player to place his queen in the center space and surround her by her six guards wins the game.

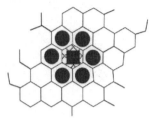

REVERSI

Reversi was developed in England in the late nineteenth century. Its rules are simple, but the strategies can be complex.

Object of the game. To have more pieces on the board when the game is over than does the opponent.

Number of players. Two.

Term.
"Capturing": Placing a piece so one or more of opponent's pieces is between a player's own pieces — horizontally, vertically, or diagonally

Equipment. Reversi is played on a board with sixty-four squares (like a draughts board), though colors of the squares have no significance. There are sixty-four playing pieces, each dark on one side and light on the other.

Reversi playing board

Playing Reversi. The playing pieces are divided in half (thirty-two to each player) and a color chosen by each player. The dark always moves first. Players place two pieces on the center of the board, facing their color up, in either of two ways.

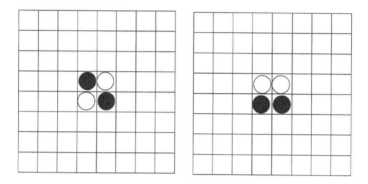

After the initial placement, each player puts one piece on the board at a time. *He must always set his piece next to an opponent's piece or lose his turn.* The aim is to capture one or more of the opponent's pieces between two of his own pieces. A player's piece may capture any number of his opponent's pieces, and in more than one direction, with one placement. A line broken by one of the player's own pieces or by an empty space is not a continuous line and is not a correct move.

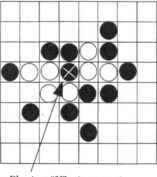

Placing "X" piece captures
diagonally, vertically, and
horizontally

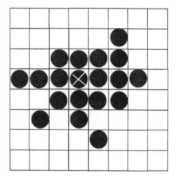

Captured pieces turned over

When one or more pieces are captured, they are reversed to show the color of their captor. In the left-hand diagram above, placing the piece marked with an X captures white pieces in three directions, causing them to be reversed to the captor's color. All the captured pieces must be reversed, even if it is not an advantage to the captor. If a piece is mistakenly reversed or is not reversed when it should be, the error may be corrected if the opponent has not begun his turn. Otherwise, it stands.

If a player cannot capture at least one piece, he loses his turn. If a player runs out of pieces, but has a chance to capture an opponent's piece, the opponent must give him a piece to allow him to complete the move.

The game is over when all sixty-four pieces are on the board or when neither player can make a move. The player who has the most pieces with his color showing wins.

NYOUT

Nyout, which has been played in Korea for hundreds of years, combines both luck and strategy. Traditional playing pieces ("horses") are carved from wood or ivory, the boards often decorated with fanciful symbols. Nyout was manufactured by Parker Brothers and became a popular parlor game in the United States in the late nineteenth century.

Object of the game. To be the first player to get all of his horses around the board.

Number of players. Any number can play as individuals or teams.

Equipment. A board with twenty circles making a large circle and nine shaded circles forming a cross within the larger circle. The points of the cross are identified as north, south, east, and west.

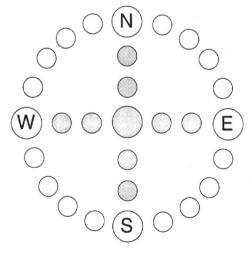

Nyout playing board

Each player (or team) has pieces that differ in color from opponents' pieces. Initially the players agree on how many horses (two, three, or four) they all will play with. One die is needed to determine moves.

Playing nyout. Players roll the die, the highest taking the first turn. Only moves up to five spaces are possible, so whenever a six is rolled the die must be rethrown. Each player enters his horses on the entry circle nearest where he is seated, the entry circle counting as one space. Horses move around the board counterclockwise.

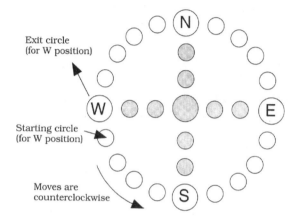

A player may have more than one horse on the ring at once; if teams play, each member may move either his teammate's horse or his own on the die roll.

When a horse lands exactly on a directional circle, it may continue around the outer circle (on the next turn) or move along the vertical or horizontal arms of the cross. If it lands on the center circle, it may make a right-angle change of direction. These moves allow evasion of an opponent's horse and shortcuts to the exit circle.

If a horse lands on a circle occupied by an opponent's horse, the latter piece is captured and must return to the starting circle and the

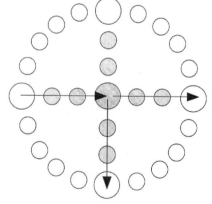

first player gets a second roll of the die. If a horse lands on a circle occupied by another of his own horses (or a teammate's horse), the two horses may be moved together in any later turns by the player or his teammate.

The game is won by the first player (or team) to get all of his horses around and off the board.

FIGHTING SERPENTS

Fighting serpents comes from alquerque, one of the oldest board games; a partial alquerque board is in the temple of Kurna in Egypt. The Moors brought alquerque to Spain in the Middle Ages and Spanish conquistadors carried it to the New World in the sixteenth century.

Fighting serpents is a version adapted by the Zuni Indians in New Mexico. The Zunis often made their boards on stone slabs or engraved them in the clay roofs of their houses.

Object of the game. To be the first player to remove all of the opponent's pieces.

Number of players. Two.

Term.
"Capturing": Jumping over an opponent's piece into a vacant contiguous space and removing the piece from the board

Equipment. A playing board with forty-six circles in three parallel rows with crisscrossed lines connecting them. Each player has twenty-three distinctive playing pieces. The board can also be scratched in the dirt and rocks used for playing pieces.

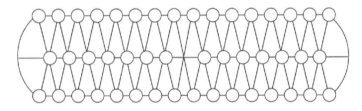

Playing fighting serpents. Each player places his pieces on the board as shown so that only three line intersections are left blank. They decide who will take the first turn.

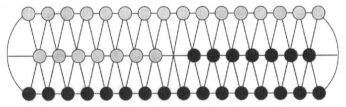

The first player moves a piece along any line to a contiguous vacant space on the board. A player *must* capture an opponent's piece whenever possible. More than one jump is allowed and direction may be changed so long as the jumps are made along a straight line — that is, jumps cannot be made around the end of the board along the curved line.

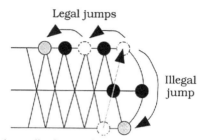

Legal jumps

Illegal jump

The game is over when all of one player's pieces have been removed.

NINE MEN'S MORRIS

Nine men's morris is one of the world's oldest board games. A morris board exists that was carved at the temple of Kurna in Egypt around 1400 B.C. Others have been found in excavations of the first city of Troy, at a Bronze Age burial site in Ireland, and in Viking Norway. In the southwestern United States, Kere, Tigue, Tewa, and Zuni Indians also played versions of the game.

The first morris boards were concentric squares with lines intersecting their sides. In the fourteenth century, a European-court variation connected the corners of the squares with diagonal lines. A like twelve-man version came to America with early British settlers. Players in the United States still use this board, which allows a three-counter row to be made on the diagonal corner lines. New versions continue to be created, especially as battle games.

Object of the game. To be the first player to remove all but two of the opponent's pieces (which disallows a row of three) or to block him so that he cannot make another move.

Number of players. Two.

Terms.
"Mill": Row of three pieces of the same color in a line

"Pounding": Removing one of the opponent's pieces from the board

Equipment. A board with three concentric squares and straight connecting lines (diagonal corner lines are optional); nine playing pieces in each of two colors. The board may even be drawn outside on the ground and rocks or sticks used for playing pieces.

Optional diagonals

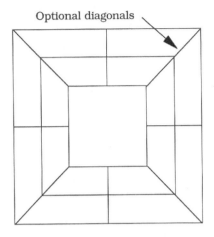

Nine men's morris board

Playing nine men's morris. The game is played on the twenty-four points (with or without diagonals) of intersecting lines. The first player places one of his pieces on the board at one of the intersections. Players alternate placing pieces on empty points, trying to form a mill, until all pieces are on the board.

When all the pieces are placed, players take turns moving a piece to an *adjacent* vacant point, again trying to form a mill. Whenever a player forms a mill (by either placement or moving), he may remove one of his opponent's pieces. He may not take a piece from a mill, however, unless there are no other pieces to take. A piece may not return to play after it has been removed from the board.

A player may open a mill by moving one of his three pieces off the line; he may close the mill again by moving the piece back to its previous position on his next turn. This makes a new mill and the player may again pound his opponent.

The player who reduces his opponent's pieces to only two or blocks all his opponent's men from making further moves wins the game.

VARIATIONS TO NINE MEN'S MORRIS

Six men's morris. Six men's morris is played on a board with only two concentric squares. Each player has six playing pieces. The game is played like nine men's morris.

Three men's morris. Three men's morris is played on a square board divided into four equal squares. Each player has four pieces; they alternate turns, placing their pieces until one completes a mill.

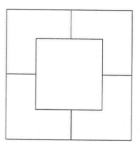

Six men's morris board

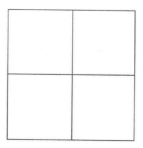

Three men's morris board

FOX AND GEESE

Game boards (England, Italy) and descriptions (Iceland) for fox and geese date from at least 1300. The household accounts of Edward IV, king of England from 1461 to 1483, show he bought two silver sets of the game. Queen Victoria and Prince Albert also enjoyed playing it.

The fox and geese concept also was popular in games in the Orient and among North American Indians. In the latter groups, a jackrabbit tries to outlast hunters or a coyote goes after chickens. The idea has even been adapted to a tag game for children to play in the snow.

Basically fox and geese is a hunt game with uneven opponents. The geese make restricted moves and depend on their numbers to corner the fox to where he cannot move. The fox, in contrast, has great maneuverability, but acts alone; he can eliminate or "kill" his opponents to cut their numbers.

Object of the game. The geese try to trap the fox so he cannot move; the fox tries to capture the geese so they cannot surround him.

Number of players. Two – one is the fox; the other, the geese.

Equipment. A cross-shaped board with thirty-three holes or spaces connected by straight and diagonal lines; seventeen playing pieces (geese) of one color and one playing piece (fox) of another color. The basic game can be played on a board or drawn on the ground outside where rocks can be used as playing pieces.

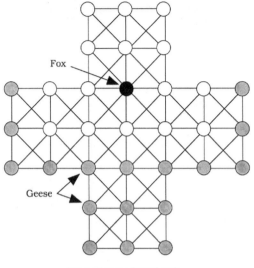

Fox and geese board with
playing pieces in place

Playing fox and geese. Arrange the playing pieces on the board. The fox is usually placed in the center as shown, but may be placed on any vacant spot he chooses.

The fox takes the first turn. He may move one space in any direction — forward, backward, diagonally, or sideways along the connecting lines. Or he attempts to kill the geese by jumping over each one into a vacant space. Multiple jumps are allowed, but the fox need not jump at every opportunity. If he has no other move, however, the fox must jump a goose even if to do so lands him in an undesirable space. When a goose is killed, it is removed from the board.

The geese may move forward or sideways one space; they cannot jump other geese. Some rules allow diagonal moves (you decide), but geese can never move backward. Geese make one move in each turn. They cannot jump the fox, but try to corner him so he cannot move.

The fox and geese alternate turns. The fox wins the game if he kills twelve geese (not enough left to surround him) or if he forces all the geese to move forward to the other side of the board so they no longer have a move. The geese win if they corner the fox.

SOLITAIRE

Solitaire is attributed to an eighteenth century French nobleman who was sentenced to solitary confinement in the Bastille. He spent his hours on a fox and geese board and developed a game for one person. The game spread to England where it became the rage. During the Victorian Era, most parlors had a solitaire board – some made simply from wood, others very elaborately crafted from other materials, such as carved ivory. Today solitaire enjoys renewed popularity as an executive toy.

Object of the game. To jump and remove pegs sequentially so that one peg remains in the center hole at the end of the game.

Number of players. One.

Equipment. A cross-shaped board with thirty-three holes or thirty-seven holes (popular in France) and thirty-two (or thirty-six) pegs. As with fox and geese, you can draw this game on the ground outside and use rocks for pegs.

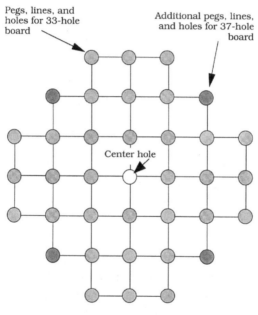

Pegs, lines, and holes for 33-hole board

Additional pegs, lines, and holes for 37-hole board

Center hole

Solitaire board with 33 (or 37) playing pieces in place

Playing solitaire. Arrange the pegs on the board as shown. Other placements for the open hole are possible, but center-hole placement is the most popular.

A peg moves forward, backward, or sideways, but not diagonally, jumping over another peg. The peg that is jumped is taken off the board. The game ends when the last peg is in the center hole. It takes concentration and patience, but it can be done!

THE GAME OF GOOSE

The first game of goose was reportedly sent by Francesco di Medici of Florence, Italy, to King Phillip II of Spain in the sixteenth century. By the end of the century, the game enjoyed wide popularity in England and most of continental Europe.

Early games of goose involved simple treks that depended on good and bad luck enroute and the roll of the dice. Boards were very intricate. They depicted religious, political, mythological, and other themes. Eighteenth-century boards displayed even more diverse themes, such as Aesop's fables (to teach children moral lessons), the French Revolution, political intrigues, the travels of Don Quixote, and publicized romantic affairs.

Object of the game. To be the first player to go around the board and reach the sixty-third square.

Number of players. Two or more.

Equipment. A playing board with sixty-three squares arranged in a spiral, a pair of dice, and a distinctive playing piece for each player.

Playing the game of goose. Players throw the dice and move their pieces according to the sum of the dice and the good and bad luck they encounter in moving along the squares of the board. If a player lands on a square already occupied by another player, the player who first landed there must go back to the square just vacated by the second player.

To win, a player must land exactly on the sixty-third square. If the number thrown overruns the remaining spaces, he must move forward to square 63, then backward until he has moved the number of squares on the dice roll. If this brings him to a square with a goose, he must move backward again the number of squares he has moved backward from square 63.

Reward and Punishment Squares

6	Bridge	Advance over the bridge to square 12
19	Inn	Remain at the inn until all other players each have had two turns
31	Well	Pay a fine by losing two turns
42	Maze	Return to square 30
52	Prison	Remain in prison until freed by another player landing on the prison square
58	Death's head	Return to square 1 and begin the game again

26	Dice	Throw the dice again in the same turn and take another
62		turn (three rolls total)

5		
14		
22		
32	Goose	Throw the dice again in the same turn
41		
50		
59		

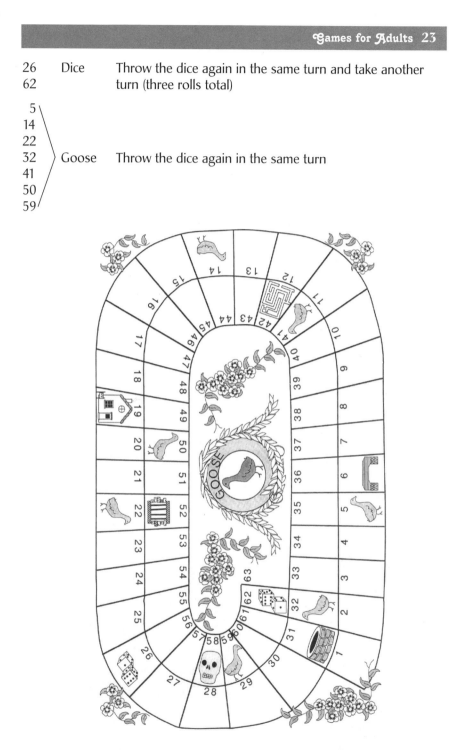

Goose playing board

SHOVE-GROAT

Shove-groat, a type of "finger billiards," was fashionable in Shakespearean England. The groat was a coin similar in size and weight to an American half-dollar.

The game was originally the purvue of the nobility; estates of the landed gentry often sported elaborate playing boards. Henry VII's household accounts record a gambling debt for the game. Shakespeare mentions shove-groat in *Henry IV, Part II*. Moreover, the game was often a target of the anti-gambling laws of the sixteenth century. By 1700, billiards had replaced shove-groat as the preferred game of the rich, but the peasants enjoyed shove-groat in the taverns. It is still a pub game today in England. Migrating overseas, the game is the ancestor of modern shuffleboard.

Object of the game. To "shove" a coin so it falls within the lines delineating one of the nine scoring "beds."

Number of players. Two.

Equipment. A playing board can be constructed as shown in the diagram. The board is divided into nine horizontal beds. Each bed has a scoring square on either end — the squares can be a writing surface for pencil or chalk (erasable) or felt for stacking discs. The brace underneath the playing surface is abutted against the edge of a table to stabilize the board during play. Sixty discs (half-dollars work well) are standard as playing pieces, but only ten are actually required if you don't use them to keep score.

Playing shove-groat. Each player shoves five discs per turn. To shove a disc, he positions it on the bottom end of the board so some of it sticks out beyond the edge. He taps the disc or strikes it with the palm of his hand or end of his thumb so the disc slides up the board to land in one of the beds. A disc must be completely within a bed to score; it cannot touch any line.

A disc that ends up beyond the beds or more than halfway into the scoring squares is "dead" and is removed from the board. A disc that lies on a line between two beds or less than halfway into the scoring squares may be left on the board, but does not score unless it is tapped into a bed by another disc. A disc that comes to rest short of the first line may be reshoved. Discs that ricochet off the top of the board and back into a bed are playable. One disc may strike another to move a poorly positioned disc into a bed. If one disc lands on top of another, neither scores. Beds may be filled in any order, but it is good strategy to try to fill the distant beds first.

At the end of each player's turn, he puts the discs that score (or marks the score) on the scoring square at his side of the appropriate bed. He retrieves the other discs to be replayed later. If a player shoots more than three discs into one bed, the excess points are added to his opponent's score (if the opponent needs points to complete that bed). The winning point must be scored by the player himself, not his opponent.

The first player to score three coins in each of the nine beds wins the game.

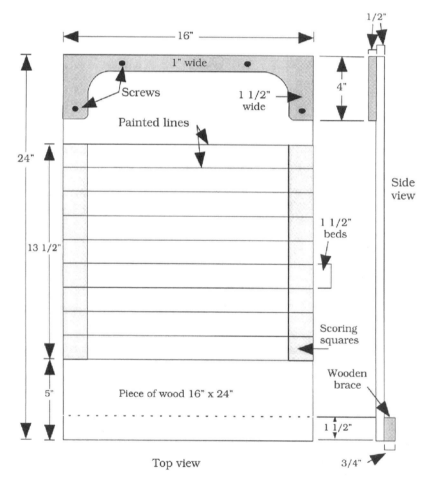

1/2"

16"

1" wide

Screws

1 1/2" wide

Painted lines

4"

Side view

24"

1 1/2" beds

13 1/2"

Scoring squares

Wooden brace

5"

Piece of wood 16" x 24"

1 1/2"

Top view

3/4"

Construction of a shove-groat board

Sand the board to a very smooth finish. Spray the area of the beds with a light coating of matte fix (to prevent "bleeding") and draw in the line with india ink. Finally, wax the board with floor or furniture wax.

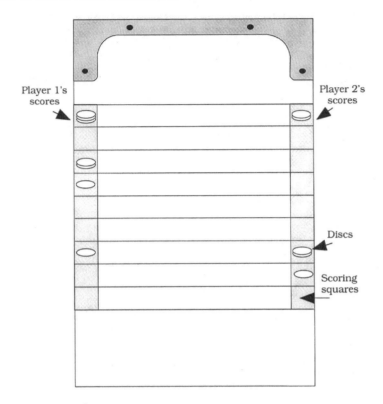

Shove-groat board with some scoring discs in place

BELL AND HAMMER

Bell and hammer is a game of chance that originated in Germany, where it was called *Schimmel.* In the early nineteenth century, the English adopted it and changed the name to bell and hammer after one of the playing cards. Fine dice were made of ivory, but some were carved from wood or bone.

Object of the game. To be the first player to collect all of the counters.

Number of players. Any number. The one who throws the highest number on the dice becomes the auctioneer for the first round. The winner of one round is the auctioneer for the next.

Term.
"Mine host": The holder of the inn card

Equipment. The equipment includes five picture cards, one each depicting a white horse, an inn, a hammer, a bell, and a bell and hammer. You also need eight dice – six dice with the numbers 1 through 6, respectively, on one side only and two dice, one with a bell, the other a hammer, on one side. Possible equipment pieces are shown below. Lastly, you need thirty-six counters for each player and one small wooden mallet or gavel. A dice cup is optional.

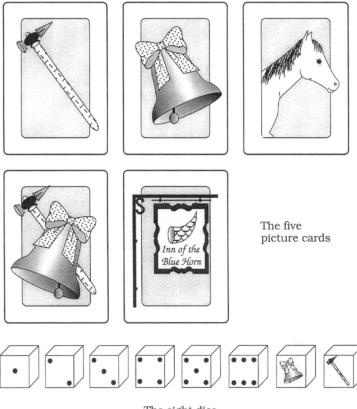

The five
picture cards

The eight dice

Playing bell and hammer. One round of the game consists of three phases:

Phase 1. The auctioneer asks all players to put four counters into a pool, then auctions off the five picture cards, one at a time; counters paid for each card are added to the pool. Only players holding cards can play each round; those who do not "buy" a card sit out the round. If a player does not have a card for two consecutive rounds, he is out of the game and his counters are added to the pool.

Phase 2. The auctioneer bangs his gavel to begin Phase 2. Each player, in turn, rolls the dice. He pays or is paid according to the following schedule:

Dice Roll	Results
Dice are all blank	All players pay one counter to the owner of the white horse
Bell, hammer, or both appear; other dice are blank	Owners of those cards pay one counter to the owner of the white horse
Bell, hammer, or both appear with one or more counters	Auctioneer pays the sum of the numbers in counters from the pool to the owner(s) of the corresponding card(s)
Only blanks and numbers appear; picture dice are blank	From the pool, auctioneer pays to the player the sum of numbers rolled
Player rolls a sum equal to the number of counters in the pool	The game ends
Player rolls a sum larger than the number of counters in the pool	Player pays the difference to mine host. Mine host "opens the inn" and Phase 3 begins

Phase 3. Again each player, in turn, rolls the dice and pays or is paid as follows:

Dice Roll	Results
Dice are all blank	Owner of the white horse pays one counter to mine host
Bell, hammer, or both appear; other dice are blank	Owners of the cards whose dice appear pay one counter to mine host
Bell, hammer, or both appear with one or more counters	Owners of the cards whose dice appear pay mine host the difference between the number rolled and the counters in the pool
Only blanks and numbers appear; picture dice are blank	From the pool, auctioneer pays to the player the sum of numbers rolled
Player rolls a sum equal to the number of counters in the pool	Player wins the round and adds the counters in the pool to his pile

FARKLE

We can document little of the history of farkle. However, a dice cup, dice, and some instructions were recently found at Fort de Chartres, Illinois, that date to the late eighteenth century when the French owned the fort. The game (with slightly modified rules) is enjoying a resurgence today.

Object of the game. To be the first player to get 10000+ points and be far enough ahead that none of the other players can pass him during a last turn.

Number of players. Any number may play. One player is designated as the scorekeeper.

Terms.
"Farkle": Any roll of one or more dice that does not result in at least one counter

"Counter": On any single roll of the dice – one or more 1s or 5s; three or more of a kind; three pairs or a straight using all six dice. A player must have at least one counter on each roll of the dice or he farkles

Equipment. Pencil and paper for scoring, six dice, a dice cup (optional). A nice substitute for a leather cup is a seed pod from a crafts store that sells dried flowers for arranging:

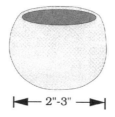

|◄— 2"-3" —►|

Playing farkle. On each turn, a player first rolls all six dice. If there are no counters, he has farkled and the play continues with the player to his left. If he has a counter (or counters), he sets one, some, or all of them aside. For example, 1s and 5s count by themselves – one or more of those rolled on one roll may be set aside. Three of a kind must be set aside together; all six dice must be set aside for three pairs or a straight. Counters on each roll are independent – dice already set aside may not be combined with dice of subsequent rolls to make straights, three of a kind, etc.

As long as a player sets aside at least one counter, he may continue to roll the remaining dice to try to better his score. If eventually all six dice become counters, he must roll *all* the dice at least one more time before passing them. Otherwise he may pass the dice at any point after a roll with at least one counter. If on any roll (including the first) he has no counters, he has farkled and loses any points accumulated in that turn.

Scoring Chart

On any roll of six dice

Six 1s	Wins the game
Six of any number but 1s	Doubles points for five of a number (below)
Straight (one each of 1, 2, 3, 4, 5, 6)	1500 points
Three pairs, e.g., two 2s, two 3s, two 6s	1000 points

On any single roll of six or less dice

	Points for one or two 1s or 5s on any roll	Points for three of a number on one roll	Points for four of a number on one roll (doubles three)	Points for five of a number on one roll (doubles four)
1s	100 each	1000	2000	4000
2s		200	400	800
3s		300	600	1200
4s		400	800	1600
5s	50 each	500	1000	2000
6s		600	1200	2400

Scoring. Each player must start his scoring by rolling at least 1000 points in one turn. He must continue to roll until he reaches that amount or farkles trying to do so. After all but one player has begun scoring, however, the remaining player is "grandfathered" in; he has no initial 1000+ points, but may begin accumulating points in his turn.

Scoring is cumulative during a turn. For example, suppose a player rolls three 2s (200 points) on his first roll and sets them aside. He then opts to roll the remaining three dice and gets one 1 and one 5 (150 additional points). Because only one die remains, he opts now to pass the dice. His score for the turn is 200 plus 150 or 350 points.

As another example, suppose the player rolls his six dice and gets one 1 and one 5 as the only counters (150 points). He decides to set the 1 aside, but to put the 5 back into his second roll (of five dice) to improve his chances for a better score. On his second roll he gets three 5s (500 points) and decides to pass the dice. His score is 100 from the first roll plus 500 from the second roll or a total of 600 points for the turn.

Sample Scoring

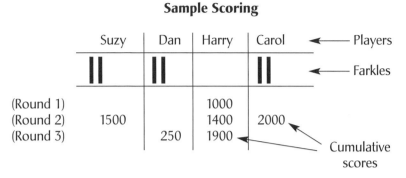

	Suzy	Dan	Harry	Carol	← Players
	‖	‖		‖	← Farkles
(Round 1)			1000		
(Round 2)	1500		1400	2000	
(Round 3)		250	1900		Cumulative scores

Round 1:
Suzy and Dan farkled
Harry rolled three pairs (1000)
Carol farkled

Round 2:
Suzy rolled a straight (1500)
Dan farkled
Harry rolled three 4s (400)
Carol rolled four 1s (2000) (because all players but Dan now have starting scores, Dan "grandfathers" in for Round 3)

Round 3:
Suzy farkled
Dan rolled two 1s and one 5 (250)
Harry rolled three 5s (500)
Carol farkled, etc.

The scorer must keep track of each player's running total *and* the number of times each player farkles. As soon as a player reaches 10000 or more points, the scorer announces the score. The other players must try one more time to beat (not tie) the high score or farkle trying to beat it.

For betting on farkle, ante and farkle amounts are negotiable. Commonly, each player must pay the winner five cents for each of his farkles and the winner also gets a twenty-five-cent ante paid by each player.

BOTTICELLI

Although this game was named for the famous Italian painter, Alessandro di Mariano Filipepi Botticelli (1445-1510), no history about its origin has been found.

Object of the game. One player (the persona) chooses a mystery "person." The others (questioners) try to determine who the mystery person is.

Number of players. Any number can play — the more, the better! The questioner who solves the identity becomes the next persona; if no one solves it, the persona stays the same for a subsequent round.

Equipment. None.

Playing botticelli. The persona decides on a person. It can be a fictional figure (Moby Dick), a cartoon character (Donald Duck), a current figure (Oprah Winfrey), a historical person (George Washington), and so forth. The only requirement is that the persona be someone not so obscure that he is unknown to most of the others. In that event, the game bogs down.

The persona announces the first letter of the person's last (or best-known) name. For example, if Leonard Bernstein has been chosen, the letter is "B."

The other players now begin to ask the persona questions. But when they ask, *they must have someone in mind that fits their question and whose last name begins with the given letter*. For example, thinking of Tony Bennett, someone might ask "Are you a singer?" The persona must respond in kind by denying being a "B" singer. He might say "I'm not Clint Black." Because that is not who the questioner had in mind, he may say "Are you another singer?"

When the persona cannot answer in kind, the questioner states who he was thinking of. If his question was appropriate to the letter and category, he has the privilege of asking a yes-no question. These may be things like "Are you an American?" or "Are you alive?"

Suppose the questioner, thinking of Bach, asks "Are you a composer?" The persona answers in kind, saying "No, I'm not Beethoven." The questioner then says "Are you another composer?" to which the persona may say "I'm not Bach." If the persona outlasts the questioner with correct answers, other categories of questions follow. Notice, in the last example, the persona has not admitted to being a composer. If the questioner later comes back to composers and the persona cannot think of another "B" composer besides Bernstein, he must confess and the game is over.

Once the persona has admitted to not being (or doing) something, no questions can be asked in that category. In our example, we have established that the persona is not a singer; the answers resulted in a yes-no question. Likewise once the persona has answered a yes-no question, such as not being alive, no questions can be asked with living people in mind (fictional or cartoon characters are never alive). As you can see, as the game continues, both the persona and the questioners become more restricted. That's why more people improve the game.

The game ends when the persona has to confess his identity or the questioners are stumped.

TANGRAM

Early history of tangram is uncertain. The most plausible theory places its beginnings in China about 1800. From there the game spread rapidly to the West. Publications about it had reached the United States and Europe by 1818; writers such as Edgar Allen Poe and Lewis Carroll were fans of the game.

The origin of the name "tangram" is also speculative. The word may have come from the Chinese, but may also be English. "Trangram" was an Old English word for a toy or puzzle. Dr. Johnson spelled it with an "r" in his 1712 dictionary. During the nineteenth century, usage gradually transformed it to "tangram."

Object of the game. To use all seven pieces to make a design.

Number of players. One at a time.

Equipment. An exact square (six-inch minimum on a side) of cardboard or wood cut into seven pieces.

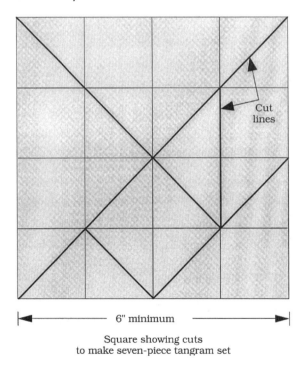

Square showing cuts
to make seven-piece tangram set

Playing tangram. The idea is to use your imagination to invent as many designs and shapes as possible. These can be silhouettes of animals, humans, cartoon faces, inanimate objects, and complex shapes (often geometric). Some possibilities are shown below. Because tangram is basically just a mental exercise, it has no formal rules.

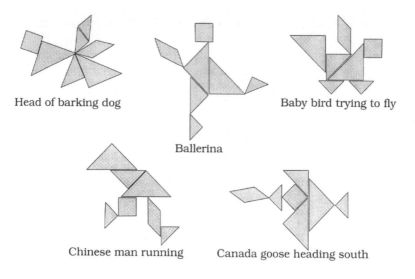

Head of barking dog   Baby bird trying to fly

Ballerina

Chinese man running   Canada goose heading south

DOMINOES

Types of dominoes are ancient and of Chinese origin. Packs were carved from ivory, bone, and wood. By the mid-1700s, domino games and modifications, such as blank tiles, were proliferating in Europe. Bone was the material of choice for early European dominoes, but by 1840 a bone strip was glued to ebony backing. Small pieces of brass were used to make tiles stand on edge. Cheaper packs, made of wood stained black, made sets available to everyone.

Dominoes is not a game; rather the tiles are the equipment to play a huge number of games — and there are many local variations of the same game. Some have simple rules; others are very creative. Three games are presented here. Two rely only on matching the spots (pips); the third introduces trumps and depends on the addition of pips.

Object of the game. Generally to be the first player to play all his tiles and score points from remaining players.

Number of players. Four for most games.

Terms.

"Boneyard": The pile of tiles from which players draw their hands

"Double tiles": Tiles with the same number of pips on both ends

"Single tiles": Tiles with a different number of pips on each end

Equipment. A pack of twenty-eight tiles in seven suits — a blank and the numbers 1 through 6. The tiles display all possible combinations of paired numbers (like rolling two dice) and the blank:

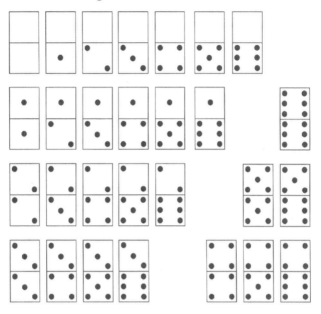

SOME VARIATIONS OF DOMINOES

Block. Block is usually played with four players, sometimes in partnerships; if two play, tiles left in the boneyard are excluded from play.

The tiles are placed face down on a table and shuffled. Each player draws seven tiles from the pile and places them on edge facing him. The player with the double-6 places it face up on the table, an end toward him. Turns rotate clockwise from the first player. The next player must play a tile with one end having a 6 (if he has one). The third player must then play to the other side of the 6 or match the number on the end of the second tile.

When two play, the player with the highest double tile places it face up on the table. The next player having a tile with a matching end then plays it. Play continues as with four players.

Double tiles are always placed vertical to the first player; single tiles are placed end-to-end. To keep the playing area manageable, a corner may be formed.

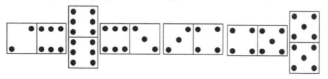

If a player cannot match either end, he says "Pass" and the next player takes a turn. The game ends when one player has placed all his tiles. His score is the total of all the pips on the tiles still in the hands of other players.

If all players become unable to play, they turn over their tiles and the player with the lowest number of total pips is the winner. His score is the total of his opponents' pips minus his own.

If partners play, the total of the pips in one partnership is subtracted from the total for the other partnership; thus it is possible for one player to play all his tiles and have his side lose the hand if his partner still has tiles with high pips.

Strategy involves getting rid of the tiles (but not always immediately if you are in a partnership!), playing high tiles when possible to minimize pips remaining, ensuring you do not become blocked on a play, and trying to create a block for opponents.

Draw. Draw is a variation of block and works well for two or three players. Each player turns up a tile; the tile with the most pips designates the first player. After the tiles are shuffled, each player draws five, six, or seven tiles (as decided) and turns them on edge toward him. The remaining tiles are left in the boneyard.

The first player places any tile he choses on the table. When a player cannot match either end, he must draw a tile from the boneyard. If the tile can be played, he does so immediately. If the tile cannot be played, he continues to draw until he either gets a playable tile or only two tiles are left in the boneyard; at this point, he passes. As in block, there is no play from the ends of doubles. The round is won when one player has placed all the tiles in his hand; he scores the total of the pips on other players' dominoes.

Matador (Russian Dominoes). Two, three, or four (as individuals) can play matador. They draw five, six, or seven tiles as they decide. The first player places any tile to start. After this, a leg is extended by making the pips on the two adjoining half-tiles *add to seven, not by matching the number of pips*. A 6 must be played to a 1; a 5 to a 2, and a 3 to a 4, and so on. Doubles are played as singles; that is if the starter is 3:3, any tile with a 4, including the 4:4 may be played against it.

No number from 1 to 6 can be added to a blank to make 7, so there are four special tiles called "matadors" (trumps). These are the three tiles whose halves total 7 (6:1, 5:2, 4:3) and the double blank. Matadors can be played anywhere at any time and *only* matadors can be played next to a blank.

A matador may be placed in one of two ways: across the line or with one half-tile in the line. If a half-tile is placed in line, only the other half-tile can be played to and it must be the number that adds to 7. If a matador is placed across the line, then the half-tile placed against it may use either half to total 7.

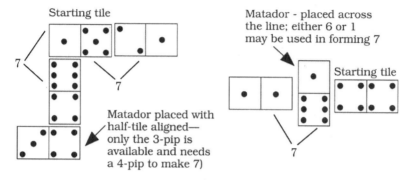

Starting tile

7

Matador placed with half-tile aligned— only the 3-pip is available and needs a 4-pip to make 7)

Matador - placed across the line; either 6 or 1 may be used in forming 7

Starting tile

A player is never obligated to play a matador. If he cannot play to make 7 and chooses not to play a matador, he must draw from the boneyard (if there is one) until he can make 7 or boneyard draws are exhausted. Then he still may pass without playing his matador.

When one player is out of tiles or all players pass, the hand ends. If a player goes out, he scores the total of his opponents' remaining pips. If all have passed, the player with the fewest pips scores the difference between the pips he has and those of his opponents. The game is 101 points.

Games
for
Children

GAMES FOR CHILDREN

C hildren in even the most primitive cultures played games. Surviving records, paintings, and artifacts show games played for centuries that are popular with children today.

Games often reflected changes in culture and values. In the Age of Enlightenment (eighteenth and nineteenth centuries), there was a dramatic increase in the middle class. Society began to emphasize the education of children and games were developed to help children progress toward that goal.

Publishing games was a logical step for book and map companies. Because children often were not allowed to play with dice or adult cards having suits – it was feared that such play would encourage gambling – board and card games were developed for the young that reflected situations in life. They were popular because they taught moral lessons (errand boy), the vagaries of good and bad luck (snakes and ladders), and basic educational facts of geography, science, math, language, and history. Outdoor games developed naturally from work-related activities and were promoted to teach agility, speed, and mental acuity.

STEEPLECHASE

Steeplechase is a nineteenth century adaptation of the game of goose. It first appeared in England about 1850; the equipment consisted of a rectangular racecourse board and playing pieces that were cardboard cutouts of horses/jockeys mounted on stands. Obstacles (jumps, ditches, fences, hedges) replaced the death's heads and prisons that represented bad luck in the game of goose. The spin of a teetotem or roll of a single die determined the movements of horses and riders around the track. Steeplechase's popularity fostered publication of many other racing games.

Object of the game. To be the first player to move his "horse" around the track, dodging and overcoming obstacles, and pass the finish line.

Number of players. Two to six.

Equipment. A teetotem or die; one distinctive playing piece for each player; a round or oval board divided into rectangular spaces, some of which are obstacles.

Playing steeplechase. Each player spins the teetotem or number disc or rolls the die. The highest roll goes first, then players proceed in descending order of the numbers they roll.

Each player then rolls again and moves his piece according to the number obtained. If the roll puts the player on an obstacle square, he loses his next turn. The first player to cross the finish line wins.

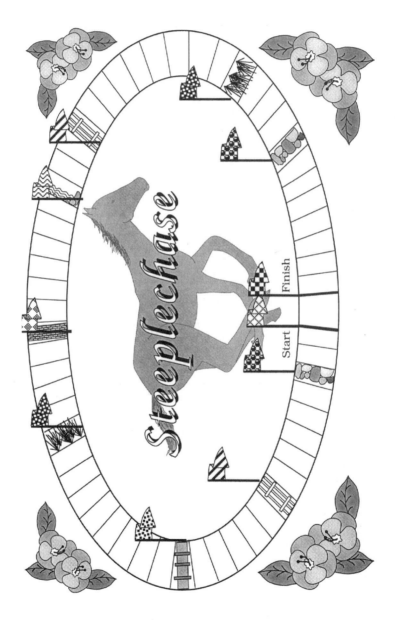

Steeplechase board

SNAKES AND LADDERS

Snakes and ladders, one of the best known children's games, is based on a game from India used to teach religious and moral concepts. Initially, virtuous deeds (ladders) shortened the soul's journey to perfection (and the journey across the board); evil deeds and bad luck (snakes) impeded the journey. The Western version, popular for over 100 years, has become just a fun obstacle race.

Object of the game. To maximize good luck and avoid bad luck and be the first player to reach the one hundredth square on the board.

Number of players. Any number.

Equipment. One or two dice and a playing board of 100 squares with snakes and ladders depicted. The snakes' heads are always higher than their tails. A distinctive playing piece is needed for each player.

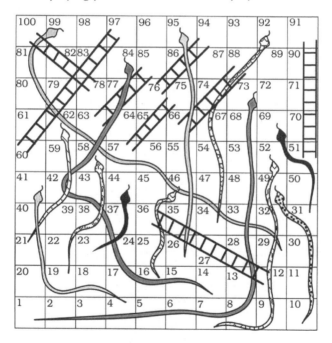

Snakes and ladders board

Playing snakes and ladders. Snakes and ladders may be played with either one or two dice (you decide). Each player must throw a 6 (one die) or a pair (two dice) to start the game. He then rolls again and moves his playing piece the number of spaces shown on the dice. Any time he rolls a later 6 (one die) or a pair (two dice), the player moves the number of squares on the roll, following the snakes and ladders if he lands on them, and then takes another roll in the same turn.

Anytime a player ends on the head of a snake, he must follow it down to the square containing its tail. Anytime he lands on the bottom of a ladder, he follows it up to the square at the top.

If a player lands on a square already occupied by an opponent, the opponent must go back to square 1.

The first player to end on square 100 wins. The last roll, however, must end with his piece exactly on the last square. If the amount of the roll is more than he needs, he moves his piece forward to square 100, then back from that square the number of excess points; the player must try for square 100 on subsequent rolls. Once the game has been won, the other players may continue to determine other places besides first place.

ERRAND BOY

Errand boy, popular in the 1800s, is typical of the proliferation of board games that were developed to teach children the rewards for diligence and good deeds and the penalties for idleness and bad deeds.

Object of the game. To be the first player to move his playing piece through the squares from 1 to 43, with incentives when he acts virtuously and punishments when he misbehaves. The goal is to become president of the company.

Number of players. Any number can play.

Equipment. A counter (die, teetotem, or number disc) to determine the players' moves, distinctive playing pieces, and an errand boy board. The board adapted here was originally twice as wide as shown (making it square), the left side being a mirror image of the right. You can make your own by duplicating the board, reversing the writing, and overlapping the row of squares containing the END square.

Playing errand boy. The players take turns spinning the counter or throwing the die to determine how far they may move in each turn. Whenever they end up on an instructional square, they must follow the directions found there.

The winner is the first player to negotiate the squares successfully and arrive at square 43. He is then the president of the company.

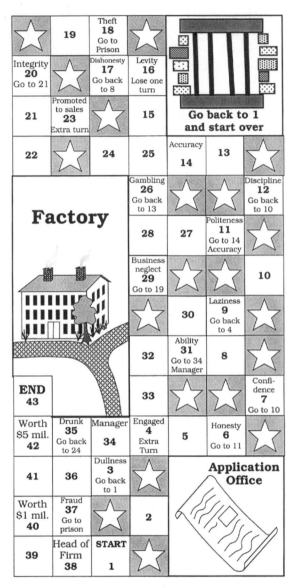

Errand boy board

SHUT THE BOX

French sailors have played shut the box for over 200 years. They probably carried the game to different parts of the world and today many variations of the game are played.

Object of the game. To shut the boxes on all the numbers 1 through 9.

Number of players. Shut the box can be a solitaire game, but playing with two or more players is common and makes the game more fun.

Equipment. Equipment can be as complicated as a throwing surface for dice with nine boxes at one end, numbered 1 through 9, and with hinged lids that can be closed to conceal the numbers inside. A simple version can be made on a piece of cardboard using objects placed over the numbers to hide them. Two dice are also needed.

1	*2*	*3*	*4*	*5*	*6*	*7*	*8*	*9*

Playing shut the box. A player rolls the dice. He may shut the boxes that correspond to the individual numbers on each die or a box that represents the total of the two dice. For example, if he rolls a 3 and a 4, he may hide those numbers or the 7.

1	*2*			*5*	*6*	*7*	*8*	*9*

His turn is over when he cannot shut a box on the roll of the dice because not all numbers or the total correspond with boxes that are still open. When the numbers of the open boxes total six or less, he rolls only one die until he has shut the boxes or rolled an unusable number.

Scoring. At the end of each player's turn, the total of the boxes still open is added to his score. He is out of the game when his score reaches 45 points or more. The winner is the last player to remain in the game.

LOTTO

Lotto was developed based on the Italian national lottery, which has been held consistently since 1530. The game is similar to bingo — which came from keno, an American version of lotto played in the nineteenth century. In the classic version, a leader calls numbers drawn randomly and players match those numbers to numbers on a card. In Victorian England, pictures and letters replaced numbers to create educational games that taught history, botany, spelling, and similar concepts to children.

Object of the game. To be the first player to cover all required sections of his card.

Number of players. Any number.

Equipment. Tokens matching the elements on the cards and a large variety of cards for players. Almost an infinite variety of card designs can be made, depending on your creativity and the ages of the players. Older children can play the classic game, while younger children need to match pictures, shapes, colors, and the like. Several ideas are presented here.

SOME VARIATIONS OF LOTTO

Classic lotto. Cards contain nine vertical rows and three to five horizontal rows. Three-by-five cards work well or you may cut your own from heavy paper. Even typing paper works, but durablility is poor. Five numbers between 1 and 90 are placed in each horizontal row; other spaces are left blank. No numbers may be duplicated on a card and no two cards should be alike. You should organize the numbers vertically; that is, single digits in the first vertical row, tens in the second, twenties in the third, and so forth. A sample card and token are shown below:

2		25			52	65		81
	15	27		43			71	85
8			36	48		68	79	

Sample card

Token

The tokens can be as simple as pieces of paper with one number from 1 through 90 on each one. Little price tags, especially those with the metal ring around them, can be purchased at office supply stores and they hold up well.

Lastly you need a way to block out numbers on a card as they are called. Scraps of paper, pennies, pebbles, or other items can be used.

Matching lottos. This type of lotto has many historical precedents and cards can be adapted for teaching concepts to any-age child. Cards may be as simple as matching shapes and colors or as complicated as teaching past events. Tokens may be anything appropriate. A version with flowers depicted on cards, published about 1872, had tokens with the popular name of the flowers, their symbolic significance (such as "inconstancy"), and their Latin names!

A simple set for small children might include about twelve shapes and various colors in random order on cards (shown below). If you're artistic, you can draw animals, household items, clothing, or other items. If you're not particularly concerned about having historically accurate materials, sets of stamps from the post office or paste-on tattoos and happy faces can be placed into the squares and tokens for matching tasks.

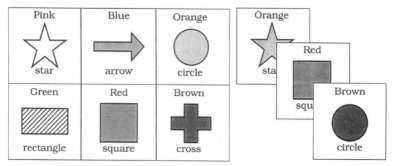

Sample card   Tokens

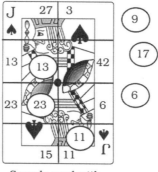

Sample card with
some tokens in place

For older children, you can use historical dates, spelling words and object names matched to pictures, foreign language words matched to pictures or English words, even geometric or chemical formulas.

Alamo falls	*U S History*		Jean Laffite roams the Carribean	1803-1806
John Adams presidency	Constitution ratified	Pilgrims land at Plymouth	Washington's winter at Valley Forge	1607
Boston tea party	Lewis and Clark Expedition	Gadsden Purchase	Monroe Doctrine	1853
Jamestown founded	Stamp Act	Paul Revere's ride	Battle of Lexington	1797-1801

Sample card   Tokens

Puzzle lottos. A final idea is to use pictures that are of interest – photographs of family members or animals, playing cards, old postcards from an antique store, etc. Cut a piece of paper the size of the picture into various random shapes. Trace the shapes onto a card and another paper. The puzzle pieces, thus made into two identical sets, act as both calling pieces and tokens to cover the puzzle as calling pieces are drawn.

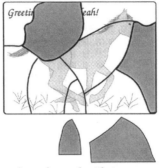

Sample card with two
shaped tokens in place

Playing lotto. Each player takes one (or more) cards and places it in front of him. Depending on the game pieces, he will need a way to cover the items (numbers, shapes of the puzzle) that are drawn by the leader. The leader draws numbers or pieces randomly from a bag or other container and calls out the result.

Each player covers the corresponding items on his card as they are drawn. The game continues until a player has covered all the required sections on his card. For classic lotto, this is five numbers in any horizontal row. For the other games shown here, it is all the squares on a card.

The potential winner calls "lotto." If the items covered are confirmed by the leader as being correct, the player is declared the winner.

JACKSTRAWS

Also called "pick-up sticks," the game of jackstraws is thought to have originated in China. Some early sets were made with carved ivory heads; intricacy determined the value of the stick. Recent sets are colored wood or plastic and color determines value.

Object of the game. To extricate each stick from a pile without moving any of the other sticks. Sticks of higher color value are sought first if they are accessible.

Number of players. Any number.

Equipment. Fifty wooden sticks (10 inches long and up to 1/8 inch in diameter). Wooden dowels are easily adapted. Each end is tapered; you can use a pencil sharpener.

The sticks are painted in five colors:

20	Yellow	3 points each
10	Red	5 points each
5	Blue	10 points each
3	Green	15 points each
2	Red and white spiral	20 points each

Playing jackstraws. Players gather around a table or on the floor. Order of players can be determined by drawing lots. One player mixes the jackstraws and gathers them into a column. He holds them just above the table or floor and lets them fall in a random pile. On carpet, it may help to brace the column in the carpet and twist the bundle *slightly*. The players use their fingers to take sticks off the pile one by one without causing any of the others to move.

Once a player has chosen a stick, he may not switch to another if the first proves too difficult. If he moves any other sticks as he works, his turn is over and the next player takes a turn.

A player who captures a red-and-white spiral stick may use it to work on other sticks that are too delicately positioned to use his fingers.

When all the sticks have been picked up, the players add up their scores. The player with the highest score wins.

NIM

Popular in all parts of the world today, the game of nim originated in the Orient several thousand years ago. It is a simple game, but takes thought and planning to win. Playing pieces can be pebbles, toothpicks, matches, or similar items. Thus materials for the game are available in most locations or they can be carried in a small container.

Object of the game. To pick up the last playing piece or force your opponent to do so (you decide).

Number of players. Two or three are best.

Equipment. Any number of playing pieces arranged in groups. A possible arrangement of matches might be:

Playing nim. Players arrange the playing pieces into any number of groups. Each player, alternating in turn, takes part or all of any group. The game is over when the last player picks up the last piece (or forces an opponent to do so if this is what the players decide).

A variation of nim allows a player to split a group instead of taking up pieces. Before the game starts, players agree how splits can be made. For example, splitting can only be done on groups with an even number of pieces, only on groups with an odd number of pieces, only on those over five pieces, or splitting a group into more than two piles, etc.

MATCH PUZZLES

Another use for matches is puzzle-solving. Three are included here, their solutions appear below.

Use the same number of matches to make three connecting triangles.

Remove six matches so that only two squares remain in the large square

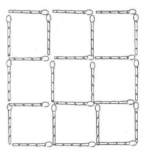

Remove five matches from the triangle below to leave only five triangles

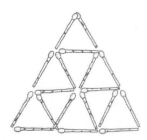

Solutions to match puzzles:

Solutions to match puzzles:

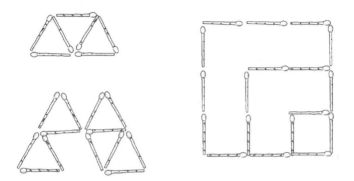

I HAVE A BASKET

Games using letters and words helped children learn language. They played the game quietly, which pleased parents, and even young children were entertained once they learned the alphabet.

Object of the game. To name items that begin with sequential letters of the alphabet.

Number of players. Any number can play; the players sit facing each other in a circle.

Equipment. None.

Playing I have a basket. The first player says "I have a basket." The player to his left asks "What's in it?" The first player then names something that starts with the letter "A." The second player names an item starting with the letter "B," and so on. When a player can't think of an object for his letter, he leaves the circle. The last player remaining is the winner.

The game may be used to improve memory. To increase difficulty, each child may say "I have a basket. In it is _____"; then he lists all the objects previously named and adds his own.

DUMB CRAMBO

Guessing games were very popular. Easily played in the parlor with virtually no equipment, they could be adapted to a variety of educational ends. Adults liked to watch and children could keep themselves occupied for hours. Charades and twenty questions continue today. Dumb crambo tested children's acting abilities as well as their knowledge of the language.

Object of the game. One team tries to guess a secret word chosen by a second team.

Number of players. Any number can play; the players divide up into two teams.

Equipment. None.

Playing dumb crambo. Team 1 chooses a secret word, such as "top," and a word that rhymes with it, such as "mop." Team 2 is told the rhyming word ("mop") and, by acting out words that rhyme with the rhyming word, tries to find and act out the secret word ("top"). When they are wrong, Team 1 hisses loudly. Team 2 acts out rhyming words until the right word is guessed. Then Team 2 picks a new word.

TIPI

Most of you probably played cat's cradle as a child. Primitive peoples around the world have played similarly with string for centuries. String games were a popular pastime among the Native Americans, including Navaho, Eskimo, Osage, Cherokee, and Apache tribes. String games have become a part of American folk culture. There are hundreds of patterns, some with accompanying stories, and more are created all the time.

Object of the game. To manipulate the string in a series of moves to form a tipi.

Number of players. One for tipi (some games, like cat's cradle, take two).

Equipment. A piece of string about 36 inches long tied together at the ends to make a loop.

Making a tipi. Hold your hands with the palms facing each other and the fingers pointing up.

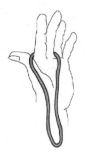

Place the string loop behind the index and middle fingers of your left hand. The rest of the loop hangs down your palm facing you.

With your right index finger, reach under the palm loop and between your left middle and index fingers. Pick up the string that crosses in back of those fingers and pull it down between the fingers and under the palm loop.

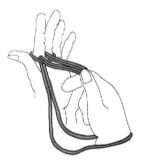

Put your right hand through the palm loop from underneath. With your right thumb and index finger, grasp the two strings coming between your left middle and index fingers. Pull the string out and down, through the palm loop as far as it will go.

Your left index and middle fingers now have a snug loop around them and two loops hang down the palm. With your right thumb and forefinger, pick up (below the knot) the nearest palm string and put it behind your thumb. Put the farthest string behind your little finger.

With your right thumb and forefinger, pick up the knot string that goes in front of the two hanging loops. Pull the knot string out to its farthest extent.

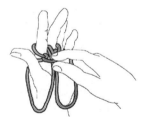

Lift your right hand, lower your left hand (palm up), and draw the strings tight. You have a tipi with two "poles" coming through its peak.

MARBLES

Marble-like games are very old and have diverse beginnings. Early marbles made of clay have been found in the tombs of Egyptian pharaohs (4000 B.C.) and tombs in Ireland (3000 B.C.). Records show marble-like games were played in ancient Greece; games were spread throughout the Roman Empire by the Roman legions. Clay marbles also have been found in southwest United States pueblo dwellings (100 B.C.) and soapstone spheres dug up from Hopewell Indian dwellings (200 A.D.) in Ohio.

Glass marbles were made in Venice, Italy, by 900 A.D. Shakespeare (1564-1616), Rabelais (1483-1553), and Defoe (1660-1731) wrote about them; Brueghal (1525?-1569) painted children playing a marble game.

From the 1600s, Germany was the center of the world marble trade; mills ground them from marble and alabaster. By the 1800s, Germany made china and agate marbles for the American market and, by 1846, mass production and intricate patterns were seen. Abraham Lincoln was reported to be an avid marbles player; milkie was his favorite game.

Terms. A whole glossary of terms has been created for marbles. They include terms for size, composition, shooting technique, game strategy, and so forth. Only a few of the more common American definitions are presented here:

"Bamboozers": Very large marbles used to "bomb" other marbles in bombing games

"Lagging": The traditional way to decide players' order of shooting. Each player stands behind a certain point (usually a line) and throws or shoots toward another point or line (target line), often about ten feet away. The player whose marble is closest to the target line on either side goes first; the second closest, second; and so forth

"Mibs" or "kimmies": Target marbles

"Mibster": A marbles player

"Peewees": Marbles of 1/2-inch diameter or less

"Shooter" or "taw": The marble a player shoots with, which may vary from 1/2 inch to 3/4 inch in diameter. Larger shooters are not necessarily easier to shoot or more accurate

Additionally there are three common methods of shooting:

"Rolling": Hold the marble in the palm of the hand and roll it toward the target. This is the easiest method, especially for small children

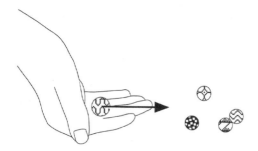

"Flicking": Place the marble on the shooting surface with the tip of the thumb behind it and the index finger curled by the first joint of the thumb. Take aim and flick the index finger quickly to flip the shooter toward the target

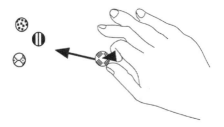

"Knuckling down": Curl your fingers and place your knuckles on the playing surface. Put a marble in the curve of the index finger and your thumb behind the marble. Aim by adjusting the angle of your hand. Shoot the marble by flipping it out with your thumb. Knuckling down is the pre-ferred shooting method for most games if players are able to do it

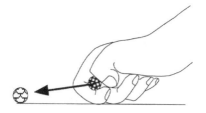

SOME VARIATIONS OF MARBLES

Ringer. Ringer is the official game played in tournaments, where only two play at once. Otherwise, from two to six can play. Play is "for fair"; that is, all players get their marbles back at the end of the game.

Object of the game. To hit a target marble or opponent's shooter, or knock them from the ring, while leaving the player's own shooter inside the ring.

Equipment and layout. The ring is drawn on smooth, level ground or hard clay. It is a 10-foot diameter circle, with a cross that intersects the center of the circle. Tournament target marbles must be glass with a 5/8-inch diameter. Players contribute an approximately equal number of marbles to make thirteen targets: one target marble is placed on the intersection of the cross and three along each arm of the cross, each 3 inches from the nearest marble. In tournaments, shooters must be 1/2 inch to 3/4 inch and may be any material except metal.

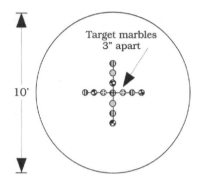

Playing ringer. Players lag to determine playing order. Tournament shooting must be by knuckling down from any point outside the ring and shooting into the ring.

When a player knocks marble(s) out of the ring, hits an opponent's shooter, or knocks it from the ring, he can keep shooting as long as his own shooter stays within the ring. After his first miss, he stops shooting, adds up his score, and the next player shoots.

If a player's shooter is in the ring after he misses, it is left there and other players can shoot at it. If his shooter is out of the ring, he claims it and shoots from anywhere on the ring on his next shot.

If a player knocks an opponent's shooter out of the ring, the opponent is out of the game.

The game ends when the last marble is shot out of the ring.

Scoring. Points are awarded as follows:

Each marble knocked out of the ring	Wins 1 point
Marble hits opponent's shooter, but doesn't knock it out of the ring	Wins 1 point
Marble knocks opponent's shooter out of the ring	Wins all points scored to that point by opponent

The first player to get 7 points wins the game.

Milkie. Milkie is a game for four players. The playing surface is a 3-foot square (or other size) drawn on the ground, with a shooting line drawn at an agreed-upon distance on one side of the square. A white or clear marble (milkie) is placed in the center of the square and each player places one marble in a corner of the square.

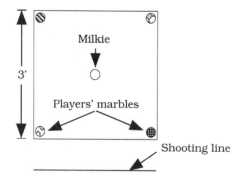

Players take turns naming an opponent's corner marble as the target and shooting at it from behind the shooting line. The shooting player (Player 1) must, however, hit the center marble first in such a way that it caroms off the shooter to hit the corner marble out of the square; the center marble must stay in the square. If Player 1 succeeds, he continues until he misses.

If Player 1 misses the center marble or if that marble misses the corner marble, one of two things can happen:

1. The owner of the corner marble (Player 2) can try to get back at Player 1 by shooting Player 1's corner marble out of the square. If successful, Player 2 moves his marble back to its corner. Player 1 must now shoot his own marble back to its original corner position, or
2. Player 2 can choose not to shoot at Player 1's marble. Player 1 then returns his marble to its original corner and the next player shoots.

When the center marble hits Player 2's marble out of the square, Player 2 loses the marble. The winner is the player with a marble left in the square at the end of the game.

Bombardier. A circle 1 foot in diameter is drawn. Each player places two or three marbles in a pile in the center. Arms outstretched, players take turns holding a bamboozer at eye level above the pile (no stooping!) and dropping it to "bomb" the pile. The bombardier keeps his bamboozer and any marbles that leave the circle. The game ends when the circle is empty.

Double ring taw. This is one of the oldest marbles games. It is for two or more players. The playing surface is the ground or any smooth surface. Two circles are drawn — an outer circle about 8 feet in diameter (shooting line) and an inner circle 1 foot in diameter ("the pound"). Each player scatters four or five marbles inside the pound.

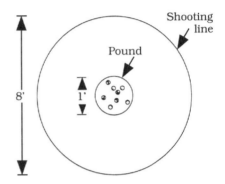

Each player, in turn, shoots a marble from the shooting line toward the target marbles. If he knocks a marble out of the pound and his shooter leaves the pound, the target marble is his and his turn is over. If his shooter remains in the pound, he must add one marble to the pound before he takes back his shooter. A shooter that ends up between the circles is left there and becomes a target marble. If a shooter comes to rest outside the 8-foot circle, the player can shoot from anywhere outside that circle on his next turn. If another player hits a shooter, the owner must give that player one marble.

The winner is the player with the most marbles when all the target marbles have been knocked out of the pound.

Knuckles down. Knuckles down is for two players. Five holes are dug, each about 6 inches in diameter and 6 feet apart, spaced as below:

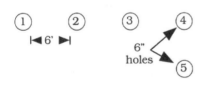

The players shoot from 1 to 2, 2 to 3, and so on to 5, then 5 to 4 and so on in reverse direction. A player continues to shoot as long as he sinks his marble in the target hole; when he misses, his turn is over. He shoots his next turn from where his marble was at the end of his last turn.

The winner is the first player to complete the course. He gets three free shots at the knuckles of the loser from a distance of 12 inches!

Marbles bridge. The "bridge" can be made of cardboard (an old shoebox works well) with arches of differing shape, width, height, and order. One possibility is shown here. Point values are assigned above the arches; the smaller the hole, the greater its point value:

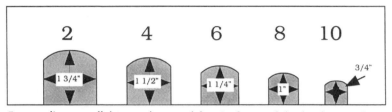

From a line parallel to and several feet in front of the bridge, each player, in turn, shoots one marble toward the bridge. The marble must pass through the hole to the back of the bridge without touching the sides for points to be scored. The winner is the player with the highest points in a given time or the one who reaches a decided-upon total score first.

Dobblers. Dobblers, a game for two to four players, is an easy game to play on any smooth, flat surface. Each player puts an agreed-upon number of marbles (in any order), but spaced about two fingers apart, along a target line. Draw a second line (shooting line) parallel to the target line and about 3 feet to 4 feet away.

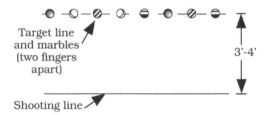

Each player, in turn, shoots at the target marbles from behind the shooting line. If he misses, his shooter remains where it is and he shoots from that location on his next turn. If an opponent hits a shooter, its owner must add another marble to the target line. If a player hits a target marble, it belongs to him.

The winner is the player with the most marbles at the end of the game.

Spangy. Variations of spangy have been played for 150 years. It can be played on any smooth surface, but must have five players. The layout is a 1-foot square inside a 10-foot circle. Each player contributes one target marble; these are placed at the center and the four corners of the square.

Shooting from outside the circle, each player, in turn, tries to knock a

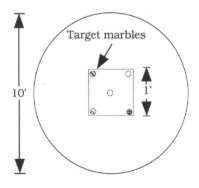

target marble out of the square. If he is successful, the marble is his and he continues shooting. If he misses the marble, his shooter stays where it stopped and becomes one of the targets.

If a player's shooter lands within a handspan (the distance between his thumb tip and the tip of his little or ring finger with his fingers spread as widely as possible), he may "span" the marbles. He places his thumb next to the shooter and another finger next to the target marble. With a single movement, he closes his hand, trying to knock the two marbles together. If he succeeds, both marbles belong to him; if he fails, he loses his shooter.

The game is won by the player with the most marbles when the square is clear of all the target marbles.

Tic-tac-toe. Marble games are easily adapted to the formats of other games – golf, obstacle courses, and croquet, to name a few. You have only to open up your own imagination in creating the necessary equipment. One simple adaptation is tic-tac-toe, a game easily played indoors or outdoors on a flat surface. Each of the two players needs several marbles that are distinct from those of his opponent. The players draw a tic-tac-toe board to the size they desire and a shooting line at an agreed-upon distance from one side of the board. They lag to see who goes first.

From behind the shooting line, players take turns shooting or tossing a marble and trying to make a line of three marbles – one in each of three squares – horizontally, vertically, or diagonally. A player may knock his opponent's marble from a square, but may not stay in an occupied square without knocking out the first marble. If a shooting marble fails to land in a square, it is picked up and reshot at another turn.

The winner is the first person to line up his three marbles. Players' marbles are returned at the end of the game.

Eggs in the bush. This is a very simple game for two players. It is a great game to keep small children occupied if they can count. The playing surface is just a hand; the equipment is several marbles.

One player places marble(s) in his fist. The opponent tries to guess how many marbles are being held. If he guesses correctly, the holder pays him that number of marbles. If he guesses incorrectly, he pays the holder the difference between his guess (either higher or lower) and the number of marbles held.

MUMBLETY-PEG

The origins of mumblety-peg are uncertain.

Object of the game. To toss a pocketknife, through increasingly difficult actions, so the blade sticks in the ground at a high enough angle that a judge can insert two fingers between the knife handle and the ground.

Number of players. Any number.

Equipment. Pocketknife.

Playing mumblety-peg. Players sit or kneel and throw the knife with their right hand unless a game rule specifies otherwise. The games go in the order given below for the longer game. Items may be omitted to make a shorter game. You may even invent some of your own.

1. **Front.** Lay the knife on your palm with the blade pointing toward your fingertips. Toss the knife upward and inward.
2. **Back.** Rest the knife on the back of your hand, blade pointing away from you. Toss the knife upward and inward.
3. **Punch.** Make your hand into a fist and place the knife handle across your knuckles above your nails with the blade toward your thumb. Twist your hand quickly to the left, snapping the knife over and toward the ground.
4. **Snaps.** Hold the blade between the thumb and forefinger of your left hand, handle pointing to the right. Strike the handle firmly downward with your right hand, causing the knife to flip over and stick into the ground.
5. **Seven Pennies.** Hold the blade between the thumb and forefinger of your right hand. Snap the knife away from you to stick in the ground at as high an angle as you can. This must be done seven times in a row.
6. **Around the Horn.** Hold the knife like you did for Seven Pennies. Swing it around your head from left to right. Then snap it away from you.
7. **Shave the Peg.** Place the blade between your first and middle fingers. If you want, you can hold it with your thumb. The handle should point away from your body and the point of the blade toward you. Snap the knife away from you.
8. **Cut Left.** Hold the knife between the thumb and forefinger of your right hand. Snap your right hand downward across your left arm, striking your left wrist hard enough to snap the knife loose.
9. **Cut Right.** Reverse the instructions for Cut Left.
10. **Headings.** Hold the knife like Seven Pennies, except touch the knife against your forehead and snap it from there.
11. **Chinnings.** The same as Headings, except hold the knife against your chin.
12. **Snaps.** The same as #4, except it must be done three times in a row.
13. **Drop In and Pull Out.** Drop the knife through a hole made by joining the tips of the thumb and forefinger of your left hand. After the blade sticks, holding the blade like in Seven Pennies and allowing the handle to touch the ground, pull the knife back through the hole. Snap the blade without changing your grip.

14. **Shave the Barber.** Hold your left hand on edge with your little finger down. Place the knife flat against your left palm, handle down, cutting edge toward you. With the fingers of your right hand, give the blade a downward snap by pulling it toward you.

15. **Lady Dives.** Hold your right hand up, palm toward you. Place the point of the knife against the heel of your hand, the handle against your fingertips. Push forward and upward, tossing the knife up and over like a diving lady.

16. **Pinwheel.** Hold your arm at a right angle to your body. Hold the knifepoint loosely between your right thumb and forefinger with the handle at a right angle to your hand. Flip the knife to the left.

17. **Kick 'Em Out.** Place the knife handle flat on the palm of your left hand, the blade sticking out over the inside. Use your right hand to strike the blade downward.

18. **Cop's Club.** Hold the knife as in Seven Pennies. Flip it toward you and, at the same time, strike upward with the same hand, making the knife spin in the opposite direction.

19. **Tony Chestnut.** Place the blade point on the toe of your shoe and snap it away from you. Repeat this at your knee, then your chest, then the front of your head.

20. **Fingers.** Like Seven Pennies, except the blade is held between your thumb and each finger in turn – two snaps are made with your forefinger and thumb and one each with your thumb and the middle, ring, and little fingers.

21. **Johnny Jump the Fence.** Stick the knife in the ground at an angle. Put your left hand down vertically about a foot away. With your right hand, strike the knife up and forward, making it go over the fence (left hand) before sticking back in the ground.

22. **O-U-T Period.** Place the point of the knife blade on your left wrist. With your right thumb and forefinger, snap it to the ground as you say "O." Do the same action off your elbow for "U" and then your shoulder for "T." Like in Punch, make a fist. Place the knife along your nails, blade toward your little finger. Snap your wrist inward hard and say "Period." When O-U-T Period is completed in the order given, the game is over.

HOPSCOTCH

Hopscotch is a very old game played throughout the world. One of the oldest hopscotch layouts is inscribed into the floor of the forum in Rome. Roads constructed by Roman legions were ideal playing surfaces and the soldiers passed on the game to European children. Hopscotch enjoys abundant variations, sometimes within cities — nearly twenty versions have been documented in San Francisco.

"Scotch" is an old English word meaning "to mark or score lightly"; children for years have been drawing the layout on the ground with stones or sticks. The game has also been called "potsy," perhaps because pottery shards were used for taws; other taws have been bottle caps, skate keys, shoe polish cans filled with sand, and boot heels. A small beanbag also makes a good taw.

Object of the game. To be the first player to complete the layout (according to the rules for each game).

Number of players. Any number; two to six is best.

Equipment. A diagram is drawn in dirt, chalked on concrete, or drawn similarly on any smooth surface. The blocks should be large enough to receive the players' feet easily so they touch no lines. Each player also needs a distinguishable taw. Three layouts and rules are presented in this book.

Playing hopscotch. Rules vary, some being relatively simple and others more complex. But the basic game works as follows:

Players, in turn, stand in front of the layout and toss their taw into the first square, hop over that square into the next square, and so on through the layout. In most games, some hops are done on one foot, others on two. At the top of the layout, players turn and hop back through the layout. The players finish by picking up their taw from the square it is in, hopping over that square, and hopping out. For some variations, on the return trip, players must hop into the square with the taw, kick it out over the baseline while hopping, then complete the rest of the squares. In some localities, a player may not hop into a square containing another person's taw; he must instead hop over all those squares and, when a player misses, he leaves his taw where it is for his next turn. Any number of hops may be taken inside a square, but a player may never touch a boundary line with his foot or his turn is over. If a player fails to toss his taw cleanly into the correct square, his turn ends and he must wait until his next turn to try again.

SOME VARIATIONS OF HOPSCOTCH

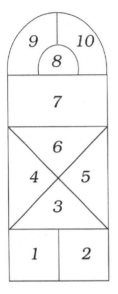

Popular hopscotch. From below the layout, the first player tosses his taw into 1. He hops into 2, then 3, jumps into 4-5 (left foot in 4, right foot in 5), hops into 6, jumps with both feet into 7, hops into 8, and jumps into 9-10 (one foot in each). To return, he turns in 9-10 (one foot in each), hops into 8, jumps with both feet in 7, etc., to 2. At 2, standing on one foot, he picks up his taw, hops on the same foot into 1, and hops out. He continues with square 2, then square 3, and so on, skipping any square containing his taw, until he completes the course or loses his turn. If he hops on a line or fails to pick up his taw, his turn is over. He leaves his taw where it is and begins there on the next turn.

The next player begins as before, but he must miss any square containing a taw. Other players rotate in turn until one has completed the layout through 10 and successfully goes out at the bottom.

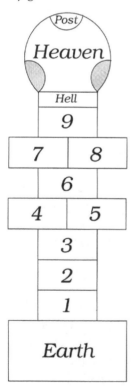

Heaven and earth hopscotch. Heaven and earth is a relatively long and complicated game. Later steps may be applied to other games as well.

1. Player stands in Earth and tosses his taw into 1. He hops on one foot from Earth to 1, picks up his taw, and hops back to Earth.

2. He stands in Earth, tosses his taw into 2; hops to 1, then 2; tosses his taw to Earth; and hops to 1, then Earth.

3. He tosses his taw into 3, hops to 1, then 2, then 3; tosses his taw to Earth; and hops to 2, to 1, then Earth. He continues this way up through 9.

4. The player tosses his taw into Heaven. If it lands in Heaven, he hops there, through each square, picks up the taw, tosses it into 9, and follows steps 1, 2, and 3 in reverse back to Earth.

If the taw lands in a side area (shaded), he may skip one of the steps 5-8 below. If it lands in the Post area, he may not laugh or speak during the game; to do so means he is out of the game for good.

For the later steps, a player:

5. Shoves his taw from square to square with his foot, hopping from Earth to Heaven and back to Earth.
6. Balances his taw on one foot, hopping from Earth through Heaven to Earth. If the taw falls, his turn is over.
7. Balances his taw on his head; hops like #6.
8. Balances his taw on his index finger; hops like #6.
9. Balances his taw on his forearm; hops like #6.
10. Balances his taw on his right knee; hops like #6.
11. Balances his taw on his left knee, hops like #6.
12. Hops through all the squares with his eyes closed — from Earth to Heaven to Earth.

In some variations a player may stand in Earth, back to the layout, and toss his taw over his shoulder. If it lands cleanly in a square, he may initial the square as his. In subsequent games, he may rest in that square with both feet down; other players must hop over that square. If on any toss or kick, the taw lands in Hell, a player's turn is over and he must start at the beginning on his next turn.

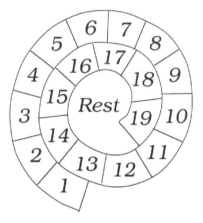

Labyrinth hopscotch. This game may be played according to the basic rules or with a ball by the following rules:

Each player hops into the first square, bouncing and catching a ball on the first bounce, then repeats the same actions for each square. After Rest is reached, he unwinds through the labyrinth, hopping and bouncing the ball as before. If he misses, he must start again on his turn. Players completing the labyrinth both ways in any one turn win the game.

QUOITS

Quoits may have originated from Greek discus throwing, but it had become a popular English game by the fourteenth century. Sometimes horseshoes were used instead of metal rings. Traders quickly spread the game around the globe. There is a Peruvian legend that the Incan king was slain while playing quoits with Spanish conquerors. The game was introduced into the

United States during the colonial period but, though still played in many places, horseshoes has replaced it in popularity.

Object of the game. To toss rings over stakes or pegs.

Number of players. Two players or teams.

Terms.
"Ringer": A pitched quoit that encircles the peg or stake

"Hobber": A pitched quoit that rests on or touches (but does not circle) the peg or stake

Equipment. For the outside game, two square dirt or clay beds are formed 18 yards apart; only one stake is used at each end. Two quoits about 6 inches in diameter are needed for each player; the quoits may be made from braided rope or heavy wire (brass rings may be purchased from a hobby shop).

You can make an indoor 20-inch square game board on a wooden block or raised platform. Painted 1-inch wooden dowels with 1 1/2-inch balls on top form the pegs. Dimensions might be:

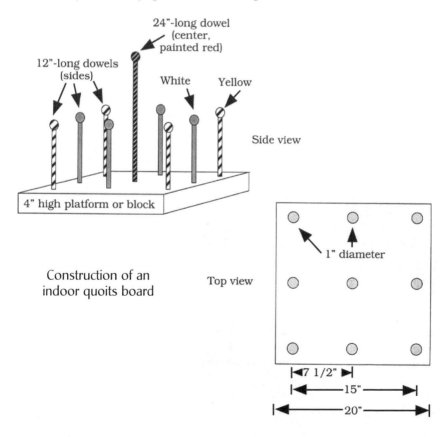

Construction of an indoor quoits board

Playing quoits. To play outdoors, one player (or team) stands at each dirt square behind the stake. Players alternate tossing their quoits at the opposite stake. Inside, players stand 6 yards from the platform and toss their quoits alternately.

Scoring. For the outside game, official scoring can be very complicated. A simplified scoring system, similar to that of horseshoes, is presented here:

Situation (by one player or team)	Points
Ringer	3
Each hobber	2
Quoit nearest the stake	1
Both quoits nearest the stake	2
Ringer and closest quoit	4
Ringer and hobber	5

Once the score for ringers has been counted, then the score for hobbers is determined and, finally, the score for quoit nearest the stake. Hobbers leaning against the stake are equal to hobbers that lie flat but touch the stake. Ties in any of the three categories are considered a draw and are not scored; that is, if each player (or team) makes a ringer, they cancel each other; the same applies to hobbers and quoits of equal distance from the stake. A game is 21 points, matches are two of three games.

For the inside game, only ringers count. One quoit cancels another if they ring the same pin. Points are:

Ringer color (by one player or team)	Points
Red	3
Yellow	2
White	1

The game is 21 points.

GRACES

Although girls and boys played together indoors, they often played different games outdoors. The game of graces was played by two girls or a mix, but two boys rarely played this "girls' " game.

Object of the game. To toss and catch a hoop back and forth to an opponent.

Number of players. Two.

Equipment. A stick for each player and a small hoop (about 6 inches in diameter). The hoop can be something as simple as an embroidery hoop or a willow withe bound together at the ends.

Playing graces. The players stand facing each other. One player places the hoop over her stick and, using the stick, tosses the hoop toward her opponent. The opponent attempts to catch the hoop with her own stick and toss it back. The players can agree on how best to keep score and determine a winner.

CONKERS

Conkers comes from a children's corruption of "conquerors." It is played throughout much of the British Empire and in some places in the United States.

Object of the game. To crack the nut of an opponent, to "conquer" it.

Number of players. Two at a time.

Equipment. A nut strung on a strong cord for each player. Horse chestnuts are traditional and by far the best. Other items, such as walnuts, hazelnuts, conch or snail shells, may also be used, but are not as good.

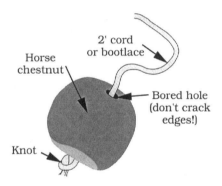

Horse chestnut

2' cord or bootlace

Bored hole (don't crack edges!)

Knot

Hardness is important; the top of the chestnut tree is thought to produce the hardest nuts. Conkers may be prepared in a number of ways, including baking or soaking in saltwater or vinegar. Tough, wrinkled "yearsies" (chestnuts stored from the previous year) are very valuable.

Playing conkers. Each player wraps the top of the cord around his hand twice. Because players believe that "strikers" do better than "strikees," the player who initially calls out "First!" takes the first shot. The other player holds his arm out with his conker hanging down about 8 inches below his fist. The conker must be still.

The first player holds his conker between his thumb and index finger. From a distance decided on by the two players, he takes aim and throws his conker at his opponent's conker. If he misses, he has two more turns. If he hits and neither conker breaks, the second player becomes the attacker. When one player's conker becomes cracked, the other player wins.

If the strings become tangled during a shot, the first player to shout "Strings!" gets an additional turn.

If a conker is dropped during play, the owner must shout "No stamps!" before his opponent shouts "Stamps!" Otherwise the opponent may jump on it. A stamped-on conker counts as a win for the conker belonging to the player who stamped.

With each win, number titles build up for the conker, e.g., a "one-er" has defeated one conker; a "two-er," two; and so forth. Titles add the numbers of the opponent's conker; for example, if a "five-er" beats a "three-er," it becomes an "eight-er."

STILTS

The origin of stilts is vague. There is evidence that stilts existed among the Maya and may have been used in some dances. Some examples also have been found in American Indian tribes. Zuni boys may have used planting sticks as stilts, thereby mixing fun with learning life skills.

Equipment. Stilts can be made in a variety of ways. Several possibilities (including some historical artifacts) are described below:

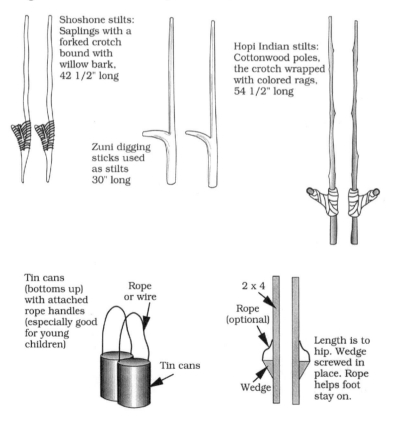

Shoshone stilts: Saplings with a forked crotch bound with willow bark, 42 1/2" long

Zuni digging sticks used as stilts 30" long

Hopi Indian stilts: Cottonwood poles, the crotch wrapped with colored rags, 54 1/2" long

Tin cans (bottoms up) with attached rope handles (especially good for young children)

Rope or wire

Tin cans

2 x 4

Rope (optional)

Wedge

Length is to hip. Wedge screwed in place. Rope helps foot stay on.

Playing with stilts. Organized play with stilts consists mostly of races, the variety of which is limited only by imagination. Players may race forward, backward, or through obstacle courses or courses with ropes that must be jumped.

Stilts also lend themselves to follow-the-leader. The group must imitate the actions of the child who is chosen to lead.

SOME VARIATIONS OF STILTS

Block race. Draw a rectangle 6 feet x 20 feet with twenty equal spaces:

1	3	5	7	9	11	13	15	17	19
2	4	6	8	10	12	14	16	18	20

Players first walk through one side of the rectangle without touching a line; they dismount at the far end, remount, and return on the other side. Then they walk through straddling the center line. Thirdly they step in every block, dismount, remount, and return the same way. You can add your own variations. Points are given for mistakes and the winner is the player with the fewest points at the end of the game.

Circular game. Draw an 18-inch circle. Each player mounts his stilts within the circle and turns completely around to the right, turns completely to the left, jumps ten times, raises one stilt and stands for five seconds, repeats for the other stilt, and walks around the edge of the circle on the line. A point is scored against him if he falls or steps out of the circle. The winner is the one having the fewest points at the end.

SNAP APPLE

Work-related games evolved from a lot of chores, especially those during the harvest. Cornhusking and apple-picking were activities that suggested a number of games and challenges to the early settlers. Remember bobbing for apples?

Object of the game. To take a bite out of an apple swinging on a string.

Number of players. One or two at a time.

Equipment. An apple on a string that is tied to the ceiling, a tree branch, etc. The apple should hang at about chin level.

Playing snap apple. The player stands facing the apple. Another person starts the apple swinging. The player tries to take a bite out of it without using his hands to stabilize it.

Card
Games

CARD GAMES

Through at least six centuries, playing cards have been a versatile medium. Their themes have reflected diverse topics: the arts, satire, wars, Lafayette's visit to America, bloody punishments, fashion, mythology, historical events, politics, and religion. They have taught their holders about heraldry, grammar, mathematics, dynastic families, and commercial products.

Despite their popularity through the ages, the true origin of playing cards is lost in antiquity. Some think cards began in China in the twelfth century, in India, or in Korea. To others, however, an Eastern origin is improbable.

A German monk in a Swiss monastery documented cards in Europe by 1377. They showed Italian suits that delineated social class — swords (knights and aristocracy), cups (clergy), coins (merchants), and clubs (soldiers and peasants). At first cards were confined to the upper classes and often were given as coveted gifts.

Many countries contributed to the development of cards. From Italy, playing cards spread to Spain where they were carried worldwide by the crews of famous navigators, such as Diaz, Columbus, and da Gama. An Apache deck (dated sometime after 1850) exists that shows an early Spanish influence — it is painted on skins with bright Spanish colors and suits.

The Germans decorated their cards with elaborate artistry; their four suits were hearts, acorns, bells, and leaves. They also perfected wood engraving in the fifteenth and sixteenth centuries, which allowed greater production at cheaper cost.

French cards date at least to 1392. Reportedly a French knight is responsible for today's four suits. Dividing the deck into only two suit colors (red and black) simplified production, lowered its cost, and clarified suits for players. The French also set the poses of the K, Q, and J in fifteenth century clothing.

England had cards at least as early as 1463. Henry VII paid out money for losses at cards. The English developed letter presses and lithography, which further cut production cost and standardized certain features, such as the double-ended court cards — now high-card holdings were not revealed to opponents.

Card-playing was recorded in Plymouth in 1633, but Americans relied on English imports until relatively late. The first known American manufacturer of playing cards was Jazania Ford in Milton, Massachusetts, in 1757.

Several companies were created over the next 100 years. The New York Consolidated Card Company introduced numbered corners in 1871, allowing poker hands to be tightly held. The Americans added the joker by 1875 and later developed slick finishes. Near the end of the 1800s, Bicycle Brand gave the court cards their happy expressions.

The Russians made no major innovations but were great consumers of European cards. The government finally began manufacture of playing cards in

1846; all profits were given to charitable foundling homes. "Biritsch" (Russian whist) reached England in 1894 and the name became corrupted to "bridge."

In spite of playing cards' popularity since their introduction, players have been plagued with opposition. As early as 1378, card-playing was condemned in Germany. The Church and royal decrees decried cards as a vice almost as soon as they appeared in Europe. Despite authoritative disfavor, card-playing guilds were formed in the Middle Ages and card-making was a profitable profession.

Cards also were an early source of tax revenue. In France in 1701, cards were so heavily taxed to support the Thirty Years War that many master card makers fled to Belgium. Taxes in England went hand-in-glove with monopolies. Inspectors of Playing Cards (Sir Walter Raleigh was one) were appointed to collect card taxes to discharge the debt of James I. English taxes on cards went up (Revolutionary War) and down, but were not abolished completely until 1960!

CRIBBAGE

Cribbage, perhaps descended from an older game called noddy, became popular with gentleman gamblers in the early seventeenth century. By that time, Sir John Suckling, an inveterate card player (and a known cheater), had standardized the rules. Charles Dickens wrote about a four-handed cribbage game in *The Old Curiosity Shop.*

Early English settlers brought the game to America. A fast-moving game, cribbage is still popular here, primarily as a two-handed game played without betting stakes.

Many early elaborate boards and tables are museum pieces. The Eskimos made boards from carved ivory to sell to sailors who came into their ports; King Gustav IV of Sweden even signed his abdication on a cribbage table in 1809!

Object of the game. To play cards in combinations that score points toward game (121 points).

Number of players. Two for the most popular version.

Terms.

"Crib": The extra hand containing the players' discards. It belongs to the dealer; its points are not known during the play of the hand, but are counted during the second phase

"His heels": A J when it is turned up as the starter card

"His nobs": Any J that is the same suit as a starter card

"Muggins": An optional part of the game (agreed on before play starts). If points unclaimed by one player are seen by the other player, he may call "Muggins" and claim the extra points for himself

"Starter": The card that is turned up on top of the pack after the deal. The starter is not part of the play, but participates in valuing both the hands and the crib in Phase 2

Equipment. A standard pack of fifty-two cards. The cards rank from K (high) to A (low). Court cards have a value of ten; the others, their face value down to A (one). Suits are not ranked.

Though scores can be kept with a pencil and paper, a cribbage board is more fun and makes the game flow faster. A simple board, like the one shown below, can be made at home or purchased at most places that sell playing cards.

Nondealer

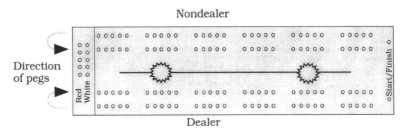

Dealer

The board has four rows of thirty holes, which are aligned in six groups of five. There are usually start and finish holes at one end and two short rows at the other to keep track of games. Accompanying each board are three distinctive pegs (two for counting, one to mark games) for each player. By convention, pegs are usually moved clockwise up the outside rows and down the inside rows. The pegs can often be stored in a small compartment on the underside of the board.

Pegging. Whenever a player scores points, he marks his score by pegging up and down his side of the board (twice around). It is customary to use two pegs. The front peg is the starting point; the back peg is brought forward from it for a subsequent score. Each hole represents 1 point. For example, suppose the nondealer scores 2 points for a pair. He moves his back peg two spaces in front of his front peg.

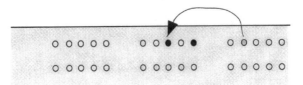

Dealing the cards. Players cut for deal, lowest card winning it. After the first round, deal alternates between players.

The dealer shuffles the cards and deals them without a cut. (This is a "gentlemen's game," so tradition says no cut is necessary to prevent cheating. In some localities, if the dealer can trick the nondealer into cutting, the dealer scores 1 point.) Dealer gives six cards to each player, one at a time, starting with the nondealer.

The players analyze their hands for the best combinations using four cards and discard the other two cards to the crib.

Discards completed, the nondealer cuts the cards. The dealer turns over the top card of the cut and places it on the top of the reconstituted pack. If a J is turned up, the dealer immediately pegs 2 points for "his heels."

Scoring combinations. Scoring combinations are as follows:

Possible combinations	Description	Point value
Fifteen	Any combination that totals exactly 15	2 points
Pair	Two cards of the same rank, e.g., two 2s	2 points
Pair royal	Three cards of the same rank, e.g., three Ks	6 points
Double pair royal	Four cards of the same rank, e.g., four 8s	12 points
Run	Three or more cards in sequence, regardless of suit or the order played	1 point for each card in sequence
Flush	Must be four cards of the same suit held in hand (starter cannot be one of the four cards, but it can be a fifth counter) Must be five cards (with the strarter) in the crib	1 point for each card of the suit

The scoring possibilities above can be combined into more complex groupings (any other scores in the hands, such as fifteens, are additional points). These combinations are:

Combinations	Description	Point value
Double run	Any three-card sequence that has one card paired, e.g., 8, 9, 10, 10	8 points
Run royal	Any four-card sequence that has one card paired, e.g., 2, 3, 3, 4, 5	10 points
Triple run	Any three cards of the same rank and two other cards in sequence with them, e.g., 5, 6, 7, 7, 7,	15 points
Quadruple run	Two pairs and a card in sequence with both, e.g., 10, 10, J, J, Q	16 points

Usually when one card is added, a combination scores as a new combination. Combinations are scored in every possible way, but only the highest combination can be scored. That is, a pair royal cannot be scored as three pairs (though the score would be the same), nor can a run of four be scored as two runs of three. What is critical is that each scoring combination must have at least one card that is different from those used in any other single scoring combination.

Playing cribbage. There are two phases during each hand:

Phase 1, Play. During play, players alternate playing their hand cards, but count accumulates between them toward 31. When that total is reached, counting starts anew.

The nondealer starts the play by placing one of his four cards on the table, face up, and stating its value. The dealer then plays a card, adding the total of the two cards and stating it. If the dealer's card creates a score, he announces and pegs its value. The nondealer then plays similarly, accumulating the total, stating any scorable combination, and pegging if appropriate. For example, suppose the nondealer plays an 8 and says "Eight." The dealer then plays a 7, adds the two together, and says "Fifteen for 2" (points); he pegs his 2 points. Then the nondealer could play a 9, saying "Twenty-four for a run of three" (8,7,9) and pegs three holes.

If a player scores a run or pair or pair royal combination, his opponent may build on those cards for a combination with a higher point value. For instance, if the dealer pegs for a run of three (5,7,6), the nondealer may add a 4 or 8, announce the total, and peg four for a run of four. Similarly, if one player has pegged for a pair of Qs, his opponent may add a Q (if under 31) and peg six for a pair royal. Also a player may score for two scoring possibilities at once. Suppose the dealer plays a 4; the nondealer, a 6; and the dealer, a 5 — this constitutes a run of three (3 points) and a fifteen for 2 points, a total score of 5 points.

Whenever a player cannot play a card without exceeding 31, he says "Go." His opponent must continue playing cards (if he can do so under 31) until he too will exceed 31. The last player to put down a card under the limit scores 1 point for go or 2 points if his card brings the total to exactly 31. When a go or 31 has been pegged, the non-pegging player plays the next card and begins counting toward 31 again. The last player to play a card from his hand pegs one hole for "last card" (or two if his total is 31).

Phase 2, Show. Both players now display their hands. Points are scored for the combinations within each hand. The starter card belongs to both hands and the crib, so there are now five cards with which to make combinations. A flush in hand can only be scored if the hand itself (without the starter) has four cards of the same suit; the starter may add one more point if it is also the same suit.

Nondealer scores his hand first and pegs his score. When the dealer has counted and pegged his hand, he does the same with the crib. A crib flush can only be scored if all five cards (including the starter) are the same suit.

The player who first pegs out at 121 wins the game.

Strategy. The most important decision for each player is which cards to discard to the crib. Because the dealer gets the crib as a second hand, he can feel free to put in two cards that may make a combination, such as a fifteen, pair, or two cards in sequence that may combine with nondealer's discards; he will get the points back. The nondealer is more concerned with retaining good cards in his hand and discarding trash to the crib. Both should keep 5s as cards that can combine with a starter of K, Q, J, or 10 to peg fifteen. Low cards are valuable to both players in pegging toward 31.

Leading and playing should also have some thought. A 5 is always a poor lead because there are a lot of chances for the opponent to make fifteen. Good leads are cards below 5 or one card of a pair — if your opponent makes a pair, you can come back with a pair royal. You must be careful as you approach 31 because combinations can only be made within the 31; they cannot overlap that total into the next counting.

Lastly, as players approach the end of the game, they should play cautiously. The nondealer counts his hand first and, if scores are close, he may count out before dealer can value and peg his hand or the crib.

A Sample Hand of Cribbage

This sample shows some of the logic for discarding to the crib, playing the hands, and counting them. Other solutions are possible. It is often difficult to see all the possible combinations when you are learning the game; they will become clearer as you gain playing skill.

The two beginning hands and the starter card are:

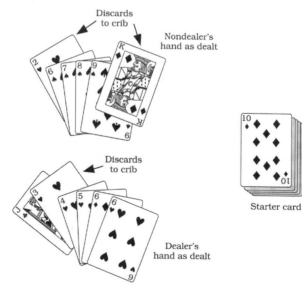

Analysis of the hands.

Both players have exceptionally good beginning hands. The nondealer has four spades in sequence and two combinations of fifteen; he has a 2 for possible pegging toward 31. Any combination with the K is a long shot and depends on the starter card; he would prefer not to put a court card in the crib, however. If he discards the K,2 to the crib, he guarantees himself 12 points in hand cards — 4 for the spade flush, 4 for two fifteens (9,6 and 8,7) and 4 for the run. Depending on the starter card, he has reasonable chances for another flush card, for a run royal, and for more fifteens. Though other discards are possible, they do not ensure a point total as high as 12, so he discards the K,2 to the crib.

The dealer, who gets the crib, has a double run (4,5,6,6) and two fifteens (4,5,6 and 4,5,6), which guarantees him 12 points also. He has a potential for "his nobs" either in his hand or the crib, so his discarding decision is relatively easy.

Phase 1, Play.

The hands might be played as follows:

Nondealer		Dealer
♠9	"9"	
		♦6 "15-2" (adding his score to the nondealer's and pegging 2 points for fifteen)
♠6	"21-2 for a pair" (adding to the total and pegging 2 points for the pair)	
		♥6 "28-6 for pair royal" (adding to the total and pegging 6 for the three 6s played in order)
	"Go" (nondealer can't play without going over 31)	
		(Dealer can't play either, so pegs 1 for go)
♠8	"8"	
		♥4 "12"
♠7	"19"	
		♥5 "24-1 for last card" (pegs 1)

Phase 2, Show.

The nondealer counts his hand first. He claims his points and pegs the total:

Nondealer's hand with starter card

Combinations	Points
Run of five	
(6, 7, 8, 9, 10)	5
Fifteens	
(9, 6 and 8, 7)	4
Flush in hand	
(four spades)	4
TOTAL	13

The dealer now counts his hand and pegs the total:

Combinations	Points
Double run	
(4, 5, 6, 6))	8
Fifteens	
(4, 5, 6 and 4,	
5, other 6 and 5, 10)	6
TOTAL	14

Dealer's hand with starter card

Lastly, the dealer turns over the crib cards, counts them, and pegs the total:

Combinations	Points
Fifteens	
(2 and 3 with J, K, and	
10, respectively)	6
TOTAL	6

Crib hand with starter card

The nondealer becomes the dealer, shuffles the cards, and deals the next hand; this time the crib is his. The game continues, alternating the deal, until one player pegs out.

VARIATIONS OF CRIBBAGE

Five-card cribbage. Also a game for two, only five cards are dealt to each player. The nondealer immediately pegs 3 points to offset having fewer chances to deal (and fewer cribs). Each player puts two cards in the crib; hands with the starter contain only four cards, but the crib has five. Game is usually 61 points.

Three-handed cribbage. Deal is decided by a cut, then passed to the left for each remaining hand. Each player gets five cards, and the crib is dealt one card. Then the players each put one card in the crib to complete it. Thus, with the starter, there are five cards in each hand and the crib. The board has three sets of holes instead of two. Game is 61 points.

Four-handed cribbage. The four people play as partners, sitting opposite each other, and deal is passed to the left for each succeeding hand. Each player is dealt five cards and discards one to the crib. Game is 121 points.

CASINO

Casino, probably taking its name from the word for a gambling establishment, is an old Italian game.

Object of the game. To capture as many cards as possible from the layout, especially those that have scoring value.

Number of players. Two.

Terms.
"Big casino": The ◆10

"Little casino": The ♠2

"Sweep": To take all the cards on the table in one turn

Equipment. A standard fifty-two-card pack. The rank of the cards is A (low) to K (high). As count 1 point, face cards have no value, the remaining cards count their numerical value.

Dealing Casino. The pack is cut for deal, the lowest card identifying the dealer throughout the game.

For the first deal, the dealer gives two cards face down to his opponent, two face up to the table, and two face down to himself. Then he repeats this so that each player has four cards and there are four face up on the table.

After the first hand is played, the dealer deals subsequent rounds similarly, but only to the players, not to the table, until the pack is used up. He must announce the last deal.

Playing Casino. Each player, in turn beginning with the nondealer, plays a card until both hands have been played. A player has four options:

Pairing. A hand card can be used to "capture" a card or cards of equal rank from the table. For example, a 6 from a player's hand may take any 6s on the layout, placing all cards face down in front of him as a.trick. Ks, Qs, and Js, because they have no value, can only be be captured by pairing.

Combining. A hand card can capture two or more cards from the table if its value equals the total of the values of the table cards. For example, a 10 can capture two 5s, a 6 and a 4, a 3 and a 7, or an 8 and two As. Like pairing, a player can take more than one combination, such as a 10 in hand taking a 6 and a 4 and two 5s.

Building. A hand card can be played on the layout to create a total that the player is able to capture with a second card in his hand on the next round. For example, if there is a 5 on the table, a player holding a 2 and a 7 may play his 2 to the 5, saying "Building 7s." On his next turn he may use his 7 to capture the 5 and the 2 if his opponent has not beaten him to the same play. A player may not make a build unless he holds in hand a card of the value to capture it. But he need not capture it on his next turn; he may make a pair or a combination (excluding his build cards) or capture a build of his opponent's first, leaving his own build for a subsequent round.

He may also create a multiple build. Assume he has made the build described above. He may also build another 7, for example, by adding an A to a 6 on the board. Then he places the two builds in one stack. On his following turn, with a 7 from his hand, he can capture the entire pile.

A player may make a build on just one card. For example, if there is a 7 on the layout and he has two 7s in hand, he may play one, saying "Building 7s," and pick up the two 7s on the table with the one in his hand on a subsequent round. If there is a 5 and a 2 on the layout and he has two 7s, he may play one, building 7s, and later pick up the combination and his first 7 with the 7 in his hand.

A player may also increase his own or an opponent's build. If he has increased the build to 7, as above, and he holds an A and an 8 in hand, he may subsequently add the A to the table and announce "Building 8s," collecting all the cards with his 8 on a later play. Builds cannot be built beyond ten because that is the highest value in the pack and a player must have a card of the rank to capture it. Increasing a multiple build is not allowed; for example, if a 3 and a 4 and a 5 and a 2 have been combined by a player building 7s, it is not permitted to add an A to one of these combinations to build an 8.

Similarly, if two 2s have been paired as building 2s, it is a multiple build and cannot be increased; if two 2s had been added for building 4s, however, then any card 6 or lower can be added to increase the build. It is good strategy to increase an opponent's build – it makes at least three cards probable winners and often prevents him from capturing the build. Builds can only be increased by hand cards.

Trailing. If a player cannot pair, combine, or build on his turn, he must trail, that is, play a card from his hand to the layout. He may trail even if he can pair, combine, or build, unless he has a build in the layout already. A player making or increasing a build may not trail while the build remains on the layout and his capturing card remains unplayed. If all the cards in the layout have been used up, the player has no choice but to trail.

Cards captured by a player, including the capturing card, are put face down in front of him. If he makes a sweep, he marks it by turning one of the captured cards face up; at the end of the game, he counts the faced- up cards to total his number of sweeps.

After the last card is played from hands, any cards still on the table go to the player who made the last capture, but this does not count as a sweep. Each deal can be a separate game or points for two deals can be added, allowing each player to deal once.

Scoring. There are 11 possible points in cards plus 1 point for each sweep. Scoring is according to the following table:

Capturing the majority of the fifty-two cards	3 points (0 if each player has has twenty-six)
Capturing the majoirty of the thirteen spades	1 point
Capturing the ♦10	2 points
Capturing the ♠2	1 point
Capturing As	1 point for each
Sweeps	1 point for each

Strategy. It is good to keep cards played in mind and extrapolate those to combinations that can still be played. This is especially true of the spade suit and As because they score points. You may want to hold casinos and As for as long as possible (even until a final trail) so the opponent has only one chance to capture them. Conversely, you should trail cards that have the potential for building or pairing in your own hand on a later turn.

Sample Hands of Casino

Dealer's first hand

Nondealer's first hand

First-hand table cards

First hand play.

Nondealer	**Dealer**
Pairs his ♥Q with the ♠Q, placing both cards face down in front of him	
	Pairs his ♥J with both the ♣J and ♦J, putting the three cards in front of him
Sweeps by taking the ♠6 with his ♦6. He places one card face up to mark the sweep	
	Because there are no cards on the table, trails with his ♥5
Trails with his ♣2	
	Could capture the ♣2 with his ♠2, a play that guarantees keeping little casino, but chooses instead to play ♠2 on the ♥5 to build 7s
Trails with his ♦3	
	Captures the ♥5 and ♠2 with the 7.

This ends the first hand with the ♣2 and the ♦3 still on the table. The dealer deals out four cards, two at a time face down, to his opponent and himself. The second round hands are the following:

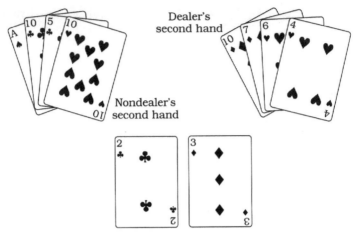

Beginning second-hand table cards

Second hand play.

Nondealer	**Dealer**
Has a decision. Can capture the ♠2 and the ♦3 with the ♣5, score a sweep, and get little casino. But nondealer is a gambler and holds two 10s with most of the pack yet to be dealt. Trails the ♣5, intending to build 10s on his next turn	
	Captures the cards on the table, making a sweep with his ♦10
Trails his ♣10	
	Trails the ♥4
Captures the ♣10 with the ♥10	
	Trails the ♥6
Trails ♠A	
	Captures the ♠A and the ♥6 with his ♦7

This completes the second hand, leaving the ♥4 on the table. At this point, the dealer has collected the majority of the cards (twelve), big and little casino, one A, and two spades that will count towards his total score; he also has one sweep. The nondealer has six cards, two spades, and one sweep.

The dealer deals the third round of cards. The game continues in rounds until all the pack has been dealt. Cards left at the end of the last round go to the player who made the last capture.

VARIATIONS OF CASINO

Four-handed (partnership) casino. Partners sit opposite each other. Captures are combined and scored as in two-handed casino. A player may play to help his partner. For example, if one player is building 5s, his partner may build a 5 for him without a 5 in his own hand. Game can be one time through the pack or four times through, which allows each player to hold all four positions.

Three-handed casino. Each player gets four cards each hand, but there are only four hands instead of six in each game. The player to the dealer's left plays first. The player to the dealer's right has a disadvantage, so it is best to play three times through the pack, rotating the deal among the three players. No points are awarded for cards or spades if there are ties for the most cards in those categories.

Royal casino. Numerical values are given to the court cards: J, 11 points; Q, 12 points; and K, 13 points. An A may be 1 or 14 points as the players decide. These values enable the court cards to be used in building, e.g., a 7 plus a 4 plus a 2 can be captured with a K.

Spade casino. This is a scoring variation in which each spade counts 1 point except A, J, and 2 (little casino), which count 2 points each.

Draw casino. Draw casino is a dealing variation. After the first deal to the players and the table, the pile is placed face down on the table. After each player plays a card, he replenishes his hand to four cards by drawing a card from the top of the pile. When all the cards have been drawn, the players play out their remaining four cards as in the two-handed game.

WHIST (BASIC AMERICAN VERSION)

Whist developed indirectly from a sixteenth century game called triomphe and directly through the English game of ruffs and honors.

Several authors helped to popularize the various early versions of the game. Whisk (sic) was first mentioned in 1674 by Cotton in the *Compleat Gamester*. The name came from "whisking" up the tricks; it was later replaced by "whist," meaning "silence!" In 1734, whist was described in the *Compleat Gamester, for the Use of Young Princesses,* by Richard Seymour, Esq. Seymour also described methods of stealing glances at opponents' hands and signaling partners with oral or gestured code.

Edmund Hoyle described the game in 1742 in *A Short Treatise on Whist.* From then on, spinoffs proliferated. Boston, an American version, was introduced in Paris by Ben Franklin about 1767. By 1810, long whist, a 10-point game, was replaced by short whist, a 5-point game, and dummy whists developed for two or three players.

By 1905 in England, bridge was the whist-type game most often played. Contract bridge came in 1926; it quickly became the dominant whist-type game worldwide.

Object of the game. To win tricks above book and reach game score of 7.

Number of players. Four, two against two as partners.

Terms.

"Book": The first six tricks taken by one side

"Slam": Taking all thirteen tricks

Equipment. One deck of fifty-two cards. Suits rank equally, cards rank from the A (high) to the 2 (low).

Dealing the cards. After the shuffle and cut, the dealer deals the pack clockwise, one at a time. The last card is turned up to determine trump. It remains face up until after the dealer has played to the first trick, then he puts it in his hand. During play, players may ask the trump suit, but not the face value of the turned-up trump.

Playing whist. The player to the left of the dealer leads to the first trick and may lead any card. The other players must follow suit if they can; otherwise they may trump or discard. The highest card of the suit led wins the trick or, if the trick is trumped, the highest trump. The winner of each trick leads to the next. One player from each partnership collects the tricks won by his side.

Scoring. All tricks above book score 1 point each. Game is 7 points. Sometimes a rubber is played (the best two of three games).

Strategy. The purpose of play is to take the most tricks. With lots of trumps, it may be wise to lead out trump before establishing another long suit (the second suit is then protected because neither opponent can trump). Second hand usually plays low, third high, and fourth tries to take the trick. If your partner leads a low card, play a high one if you have one (unless the intervening opponent's card is higher). A partner's suit lead should be returned at the first chance to do so unless you have a suit of your own to establish or a return of his suit is clearly unwise.

EUCHRE

The ancestry of euchre is old, but its origins are vague. One view holds that it came from the Spanish game of triomphe (mentioned as early as 1520). According to this theory, it was modified in France and introduced to America by the French in Louisiana. A second belief is that euchre had a more mixed beginning, possibly originating from the Irish game of spoil five and undergoing many changes.

Object of the game. To win the most tricks (at least three).

Number of players. Four, two against two as partners. It can also be played by two as individuals or by three, with the two opponents temporarily as partners against the player making trump.

Terms.

"At the bridge": Having 4 points

"Crossing it": Naming trump the opposite color of the original turn-up

"Cross suits": The two suits of opposite color from the trump suit

"Euchre": Failure by the side making trump to take at least three tricks

"Left bower": J of the same color as the right bower

"Making it next": Naming trump the same color as the original turn-up

"Next suit": The suit that is the same color as the trump suit

"Right bower": J of the trump suit

"Winning the march": Taking all five tricks

Equipment. A thirty-two-card pack – a standard deck with 6s, 5s, 4s, 3s, and 2s removed. Sometimes a twenty-eight-card pack (7s omitted) or a twenty-four-card pack (8s omitted) is used. The joker may be added.

The cards rank from A (high) down to 7 (low) except in the trump suit. In that suit, the right bower is the highest trump; the second highest trump is the left bower and, if the joker is used, it is the highest trump of all (higher than either bower). Therefore, the trump suit contains nine cards (ten with the joker); the "next suit" has seven cards; and the "cross suits" contain eight cards.

Dealing the cards. The dealer shuffles, the opponent cuts. Dealing clockwise to his left, the dealer gives each player five cards in two groups – of two, then three; or three, then two.

The pack is then placed face down on the table and the top card turned up to fix the trump. If the card turned up is the joker (if used), the dealer chooses the suit it represents before looking at his cards. Or the suit for the joker may be decided before the deal; in past times, it was considered to be a spade.

Making the trump. The players, in turn, can accept or reject the proposed trump. If accepted, the card becomes part of the dealer's hand, but he leaves it on top of the pack until he plays it. He must, however, immediately discard a card, placing it face down beneath the undealt pack.

The player to the dealer's left has the first chance to accept the trump by saying "I order it up." To reject the trump, he says "I pass." Dealer's partner may now accept the trump by saying "I assist" or pass. If he passes, the player on the dealer's right may "order it up" or pass. If he passes, the dealer may accept (by discarding a card under the pack) or reject the trump by placing the turned-up card face down crosswise beneath the pack.

If all reject the trump suit, the player on the dealer's left names any of the other three suits as trump or passes. If he passes, the other players, in turn, have the same opportunity. If all four players pass the second round, the cards are thrown in and the deal passes to the next player.

The player who makes trumps, whether he accepts the turn-up or names trump himself, has the right to go alone. If he chooses that option, he must announce it before the first lead. His partner cannot object, but lays his cards face down on the table and does not participate in the play. Tricks then consist of only three cards and points won or lost are given to the partnership.

If a player revokes (fails to follow suit when he can) and the trick has been completed, the hands are abandoned and a revoke scored.

Playing euchre. The opening lead comes from the player to the left of the dealer, unless the player making the trump is playing alone – then the player to the left of the lone player leads first. Players must follow the suit of the card led. If they cannot, they may play any card – trump or discard. There is no obligation to win the trick. The trick is won by the highest card of the suit led (if no one trumps) or the highest trump. The winner of a trick leads to the next. Each trick is kept by the player taking it; tricks cannot be reexamined until the hand is over.

Scoring. The partnership making trumps scores 1 point for three or four tricks and 2 points for winning the march. If the maker plays alone, his side scores 1 point for three or four tricks and 4 for winning the march. If the making side is euchred, the opponents score 2 points.

If a player revokes (and the trick is completed), the hands are abandoned and the erring player's opponents score 2 points. If the revoke is against a lone player, the lone player's side scores 4 points.

The game is 5 (usual), 7, or 10 points as agreed. Each side keeps its own score with unused cards as shown to your right:

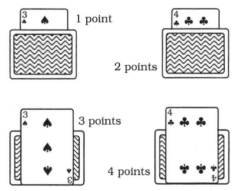

Strategy. The primary decision is whether or not to make trumps. Since the trump suit has nine (or ten) cards, an average of more than five trumps will be dealt into the players' hands. The dealer is likely to gain a second trump when it is ordered up. Therefore the dealer's opponents should not order up the trump without three fairly sure tricks — and even with them, it may not be the best idea. If the dealer's first opponent is strong in the suit of the same color as the turn-up, especially if he has the left bower, waiting until the second round will keep the dealer from gaining a second trump. If the dealer's side names trump, the player to his left is likely to euchre the dealer's side.

The dealer may want to take up the trump when his opponents have 4 points to prevent them from naming trump.

Dealer's partner can assist with two side As or with one side A and two trumps; the turn-up should give the dealer enough trumps for partnership control. If the turn-up is a high card, especially a bower, he may pass to give the dealer a chance to play alone.

Scoring impacts decisions. If one side is at the bridge and the opponents have 2 points or less, even if the side is euchred, it will not cost them the game. A player at the bridge often will order up trump to stop one of his opponents from making it alone.

When the dealer turns down the trump, he probably does not have a bower. The player to his left will usually "make it next" if he can. The dealer's partner prefers to "cross," however. *But, in all cases, a player holding three sure tricks should name the trump.*

For playing alone a player requires three probable tricks and the possibility for five: for instance, a hand with the two top trumps and two As or an A and a third trump. Playing alone may be a good defense with a weak hand if the opponents are at the bridge and the player's side has few points.

Only two real decisions can occur during play. A player with the top trump cards should draw trump early. Players should take tricks whenever they can.

VARIATIONS OF EUCHRE

Two-handed euchre. The play of two-handed euchre is the same, except that the 8s and 7s are removed from the deck. A euchre scores 2 points and making a march scores 2 points.

Three-handed euchre. Three-handed euchre also is played the same way; each plays for himself, but two players combine in a temporary partnership to oppose the player making trump. A euchre counts 2 points (to each partner). Taking three or four tricks scores 1 point for the maker of trump; winning a march scores 3 points. The first player to reach 5 points wins the game.

ECARTÉ

Ecarté is a euchre-type game. It is descended from the old Spanish game of triomphe, the French game of french ruff, and many later modifications. At one time, ecarté was regarded as the national card game of France.

Object of the game. To win the most tricks.

Number of players. Two.

Terms.
"Making the trick": Taking the majority of tricks (at least three)

"Making the vole": Taking all five tricks

Equipment. A thirty-two-card pack — a standard deck with 6s, 5s, 4s, 3s, and 2s removed. Suits are of equal rank; the cards in each suit rank K (high), Q, J, A, 10, 9, 8, 7 (low).

Dealing the cards. Both players can shuffle, the dealer last. The non-dealer cuts. Dealer gives five cards to the nondealer and himself in two groups — of two, then three; or three, then two. The order he chooses remains for the rest of the game.

The eleventh card is turned up to fix the trump suit. The rest of the pack is put beside it for the draw pile. The dealer scores 1 point immediately if the turned-up card is a K.

Arriving at the hands. The nondealer takes the first action. If he wants to play his original hand, he says "I play." If he wants to try for a stronger hand by replacing some cards, he says "I propose." The dealer may refuse his proposal by saying "Play" or accept it by saying "Accept." If the proposal is accepted, each player may discard cards from his hand and replace them from the top of the pile. The nondealer goes first and must exchange at least one card; the dealer then may exchange from no cards to five cards. Discards are faced down and cannot be examined. The trump card remains in view face up and is never taken into a hand.

After the first draws, the nondealer may play or propose again and dealer may again refuse or accept. This is repeated until one player says "Play" or the pile is used up. If at the end there are not enough cards to satisfy a player, he may exchange only the number of cards remaining.

Playing ecarté. A player holding the K of trumps scores 1 point if he announces it before the first lead is made (he may forfeit the point by not announcing it if he wishes to keep his holding secret).

The nondealer opens the lead, stating its suit. Each player must follow the suit led if possible and *must win the trick if he can*, either by playing a higher card in the suit led or by trumping if he is void in the suit led. If he has neither the suit nor a trump, he may discard.

The winner of each trick leads to the next and announces the suit. If the suit is misstated on any lead, the other player may demand that the lead remain or that it be taken back and a card of the stated suit be led. If the erring player has no card of the stated suit, the other player may name a suit to lead.

Renounce: If a player does not win a trick when possible or follow suit, the cards are taken up and the hand replayed. If the erring player does not take all five tricks, he does not score; taking five tricks earns him 1 point only.

Tricks are turned face down when taken and may not be reexamined.

Scoring. The trump K turned up is a point for the dealer; held in hand the trump K is a point for either player if it is announced before the first lead.

For playing hands originally dealt. The player who decides to play scores 1 point for making the trick or 2 points for making the vole. If he fails to take at least three tricks, his opponent scores 2 points (no bonus for vole).

For playing hands once a proposal has been accepted. Either player who is successful scores 1 point for making the trick and 2 for making the vole.

Maximum points on any deal are 3 − 2 for vole and 1 for the K of trumps. Game is 5 points. A player with 4 points who is dealt the K of trumps may expose it immediately to win.

Strategy. Judgment is minimal because a player must win a trick if he can. The most important decisions are whether to play, propose, or accept. The player playing a dealt hand should play only if his chances of taking the majority of tricks are 2:1 or better. Minimum hands which offer those odds are called *jeux de regle* hands. Examples of *jeux de regle* hands are (diamonds trump):

1. Any hand with four or five trumps

2. Any hand with three trumps and any two cards in one outside suit

3. Any hand with two trumps and at least:
   K,7 in one outside suit; 9 in another
   A,10 in one outside suit; A in another
   J,J,J in differing suits, or
   Q,Q,7 in differing suits

4. Any hand with one trump and at least:
   K,x,x,x in one outside suit
   K,Q,x in one outside suit
   K,x,x in one outside suit, K in another
   Two two-card outside suits headed by K,A
       and K,7; or Q,J and Q,A
   If the cards in outside suits are split into three
       suits, the doubleton must be headed by K
       or Q,J; one singleton must be K

5. Any hand with no trumps
   Three outside suits headed by K; or Q,J

The opening lead is very important and the player leading has a small advantage. When three Ks or trumps are held, it is better to play, not propose (unless there is a chance to improve the hand to make vole); the hand is already strong enough to prevent the other player from making vole. When discarding to the pile, it is best to keep Ks and trumps.

PIQUET

Piquet is an ancestor to several modern games, including pinochle. Some scholars believe in a Spanish origin; others postulate piquet first appeared in France during the reign of Charles VII (1422-1461). In any case, it was played in Elizabethan England as cent, sand, or saint. Though complicated at first because it combines melding with trick-taking, once learned, piquet is a very challenging and fun game.

Object of the game. To score initially for certain combinations held in the hand, then to win tricks, eventually adding up enough points to reach 100.

Number of players. Two.

Terms.

"Capot": All twelve tricks taken by one player during the play

"Talon": The eight cards remaining after the deal

Equipment. A thirty-two-card pack — A (high), K, Q, J, 10, 9, 8, and 7 (low) in each suit; suits rank equally.

Dealing the cards. Each player is dealt twelve cards in groups of either two or three. The talon is placed face down. Some play that the top five cards are placed across the top of the bottom three, but this is not a rule.

Establishing the hands. The players look at their hands. If the non-dealer has no K, Q, or J, he announces a "carte blanche" and scores 10 points immediately. The dealer cannot announce a carte blanche until his opponent has discarded.

The nondealer now exchanges from one to five of his cards by discarding them face down and drawing the same quantity of cards from the top of the talon. He must exchange at least one card. If he exchanges less than five, he may look at those he was entitled to draw, but didn't, and put them back on the top of the talon. He does not show the cards to the dealer.

The dealer announces a carte blanche (if he has one) and then discards and draws to replace his discards (up to five cards) from the top of the talon. He may take none (American rules say he must take at least one, though this may be waived).

Some rules say the dealer may look at the cards he leaves, but if he does, the nondealer may look at them also after he has led to the first trick. Other rules say the dealer may turn up the cards remaining after the discard for both players to see or leave them hidden. In the latter case, each player may look at his own discards at any point in the game.

Playing piquet. The game consists of two phases: points before the play and the play.

Phase 1, Points before the play. The hands are compared and scored in three ways in the order given below. A player can be asked to show the cards for which he is scoring in any category, but this is seldom done because each player can guess from his own holdings what his opponent holds.

1. The point. The nondealer states "Point of ___ ," the blank containing the number of cards in his longest suit. If this is longer than the dealer's longest suit, the dealer says "Good." If it is shorter, the dealer says "Not good." If the dealer's suit is equal in length, he asks "Making?" telling the nondealer to count up the value of each card in the suit, where:

A = 11 points
K, Q, J = 10 points each
Number cards = face value (optional rule)

If the total surpasses that of the dealer, he says "Good"; if not, "Not good" or "Equal."

The player with the longer suit (or, failing that, the higher point value) scores 1 point for each card in his suit. If the total is equal in both hands, neither scores.

2. Sequences (three or more cards of the same suit in sequence). The nondealer announces the number of cards in his longest sequence, using the French terms for the quantities:

tierce (3)   sixtieme (6)
quart (4)   septieme (7)
quinte (5)   huitieme (8)

The dealer responds "Good" or "Not good" or, if his longest sequence is the same length, "How high?" The nondealer states the highest card in his sequence and the dealer says "Good," "Not good," or "Equal."

The player with the best sequence scores:

tierce = 3 points
quart = 4 points
quinte or more = 10 points + 1 for each card

The player with the best sequence may score also for any additional sequences he holds.

3. Quatorzes and trios (any four of a kind; three of a kind above 9s). The nondealer announces the rank of his highest quatorzes or, if he has none, his highest trio. The dealer states "Good" or "Not good."

The player holding the higher quatorze scores 14 points, or if neither player holds one, the highest trio scores 3 points. If neither holds a quatorze or trio, no points are given.

The player who scores for quatorzes or trios may score for lesser ones as well.

Sinking. In some variations of piquet, to mislead his opponent, a player need not claim his best combination in a category. For example, a player holding a quatorze of Ks may announce a trio. If his opponent asks to see them, the player can choose any three. More often the opponent will ask which K is *not* being declared and the player may name any one. If he declares a lower combination, however, he can only score for that.

Summary. In scoring points before the play, only the better point value is scored, only the longer (or higher card) sequence wins. The player who scores the winning sequence or the winning quatorze or trio may score others.

Phase 2, The play. Before play begins, the nondealer states his summary score for carte blanche (if any) and the three categories above. Leading to a trick scores 1 point, so he adds 1, states his new score, and leads to the first trick.

The dealer states his total for carte blanche (if any) and the three categories before play and plays to the first trick. Thereafter, each player states his score aloud, updating his total every time he plays a card.

Each player must follow the suit led if he can. If he cannot, he may play any card. The higher card of the suit led wins the trick and the player who takes the trick leads to the next.

Players score 1 point for each lead they make. A player who wins a trick led by his opponent scores 1 point. If the nondealer wins the last trick, he scores 1 additional point for a total of 2 points for the trick.

The player who takes most of the tricks gets 10 points ("ten for the cards"). If each take six tricks, neither scores extra points. A player who takes capot scores an extra 40 points instead of 10.

There are two extraordinary scores besides carte blanche and capot. If a player scores 30 points in the combinations *before play and in play* before his opponent scores even 1 point, he scores "pique," which gives him an extra 30 points. Suppose the nondealer scores 1 point for carte blanche, 5 points for point, 5 for sequence, 14 for quatorze, 3 for trio, and makes the first two leads (2 points): his total is 30, giving him pique, so his score jumps immediately to 60. Because the nondealer scores 1 point for the first lead, the dealer can never score pique.

If a player scores 30 points *in hand combinations only* before his opponent scores even 1 point, he has "repique," giving him an extra 60 points. Suppose the dealer scores 6 points for point, 17 for a septieme (10 + 7) sequence, and 14 for quatorze, he now has 37 points and his score becomes 97.

Strategy. Most of the strategy lies in discarding and which cards to discard depends on who is dealing.

Each player must try to decide what the other holds. If a player is void in a suit, it stands to reason the other may be long in that suit. In that case, scoring for point is not practical and he should mold his hand to score in other categories.

The nondealer should take a strong offensive position. He cannot have pique against him (the opening lead gives him a point). Leading first gives him an advantage in trick-taking and he can exchange five cards to the dealer's three. He should try to keep high cards for hand entry and build a long suit to run during play.

The dealer, in contrast, must discard for a defensive advantage. A long suit doesn't help if he may never get the lead or may have to discard from his length before he gets the lead. A better strategy for the dealer is to keep stoppers in two or three suits: protected Qs (Q,x,x), protected Ks (K,x), and As.

Consider the hand to your right. The nondealer may think about discarding the ♠K, ♠7, ♣Q, ♣J, and ♣8. One more heart would ensure he makes most of the tricks and he has a chance of scoring for both point and sequence.

The dealer, with the same hand, might discard the ♥10, ♥8, and ♥7. That choice lets him keep stoppers in all suits. If he throws away a club or a spade, the nondealer's high cards might pick up his ♣Q or ♠K and take more tricks.

A Sample Game of Piquet

This sample illustrates some of the logic in discarding and playing the game of piquet. Other solutions are possible. Because piquet is a rather complex game (especially at the beginning!), you should persevere – your options and the sense of the game will become clearer as you play.

The two beginning hands are as follows:

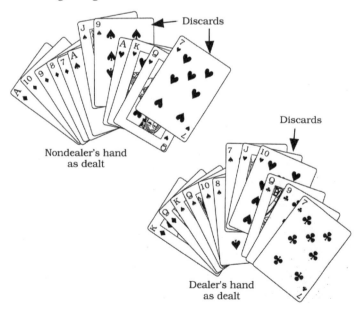

Nondealer's hand
as dealt

Discards

Discards

Dealer's hand
as dealt

Analysis of the hands.

Neither player has a carte blanche.

The nondealer has a good starting hand. He has a long diamond suit that he may be able to run and he has stoppers in two other suits (the ♠A and the high hearts). Should he draw the fourth A, he would have excellent control of all suits. His opportunities for taking tricks depend on adding to his diamonds and he has good chances for scoring point and sequence with hearts. He therefore keeps his diamonds, high hearts, and As, discarding the ♥7, ♠9, and ♠J. For his three discards, he draws the ♦J, ♥9, ♣A.

The dealer has a weaker hand initially, but one with enough possibilities to probably prevent a pique, repique, or capot being scored against him. He has stoppers in three suits (protected ♦K, ♠K, ♣Q). He may be able to add to his length in spades and there is a chance (albeit slim!) for a trio of Qs to score points. He decides the best defense is to keep his three Qs and his stoppers. He discards the ♠7, ♥J, and ♥10. He draws luckily, gaining the ♣K, ♣J, and ♣10.

After the draw, the hands look like:

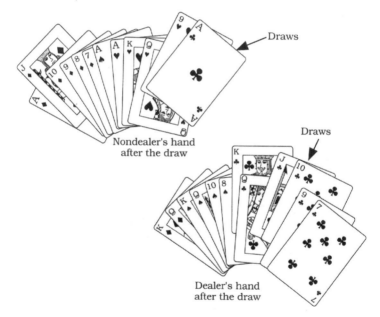

Nondealer's hand after the draw

Draws

Draws

Dealer's hand after the draw

The scoring for combinations before the play is:

Nondealer:	"Point of six." (six diamonds)
Dealer:	"Making?" (equal length in clubs)
Nondealer:	"55." (♦A,J,10,9,8,7 added together = 55)
Dealer:	"Not good." (♣K,Q,J,10,9,7 = 56).

Nondealer:	"Quinte." (run of five diamonds, J high)
Dealer:	"How high?" (run of five clubs, K high)
Nondealer:	"Jack."
Dealer:	"Not good."
Nondealer:	"Quatorze."
Dealer:	"Good." (He has no quatorze; his K and Q trios do not count)

Nondealer now states his score: "Quatorze, 14. I start with 14." He leads the first card (the ♦7) and says "15" (adding 1 point for lead).

Dealer states his score: "Point of six is 6 and quinte is 15; I start with 21." He plays to the first trick and wins it with the ♦Q, saying "22" (adding 1 point for taking a trick led by his opponent).

An example of how the tricks of the hand might be played is given below. The winner of each trick has an * by the trick and leads to the next trick.

The nondealer has many prospects for tricks and control of all suits (As). He leads low from his long suit to force out one missing court card while he still has control.

Nondealer			**Dealer**	
♦7	"15" (lead point)	⟶ *	♦Q	"22" (takes opponent's lead)
* ♣A	"16" (takes opponent's lead) ⟵		♣7	"23" (lead point)
* ♦A	"17" (lead point) ⟶		♦K	"23"
* ♦J	"18" etc. ⟶		♠8	"23"
* ♦10	"19"		♠10	"23"
* ♦9	"20"		♣9	"23"
* ♦8	"21"		♣10	"23"
* ♠A	"22"		♠Q	"23"
* ♥A	"23"		♣J	"23"
* ♥K	"24"		♣Q	"23"
* ♥Q	"25"		♣K	"23"
♥9	"26 and 10 for the cards makes 36"		♠K	"23"

Games for Gamblers

GAMES FOR GAMBLERS

From the dawn of time, men have made decisions by appealing to chance. Records of games — and gambling — are found in the earliest civilizations. Early gambling was simple. People tossed coins, bet on races, and cast dice or bones. Playing cards provided a convenient and sophisticated means of gambling.

Some more (and less) notable historical figures have made their mark as gamblers. The stories may be apocryphal, but the characters give us much of the stuff of legend. For example:

• The Earl of Sandwich, playing at White's club in London, once requested a meal be delivered to his table so play would not be interrupted. His order was meat between two pieces of bread — the first "sandwich."

• Edward Pendleton, a rascal in Washington before the Civil War, had a gambling establishment called the "hall of the bleeding heart" by those he duped. He employed beautiful "lady lobbyists" who socialized frequently with congressmen!

• James Ashby was a card enthusiast who passed signals to his gaming partner by playing his violin.

• Gambling was immensely popular on the Mississippi steamboats; by 1850, there were 500 boats and at least 1,000 swanky gamblers. Price McGrath, who learned gaming on Mississippi riverboats, set up a house in New Orleans where even his lowest hirelings wore evening clothes.

• Two planters began a poker game in Austin, Texas, in 1853. They played through the Civil War and Reconstruction until 1873, when they both died at the same time.

• Doc Holliday made more at Wyatt Earp's saloon in Tombstone, Arizona, than he did with his guns.

• Poker Alice Tubbs kept order with a six-shooter in her saloons.

• Wild Bill Hickok sat in on a poker game in Saloon No. 10 in Deadwood, South Dakota, in 1876. He did not sit as usual with his back to the wall and his face toward the door. He had just drawn cards when Jackie McCall entered and shot Hickok in the head. McCall had been hired by gamblers who anticipated that Hickok would be made marshal of Deadwood and, as such, would curtail their game. Hickok's hand, the infamous "dead man's hand," contained the two black As and the two black 8s; the fifth card is contested, but is thought to have been either the ♦Q or ♦J.

• Emma (Eleanora) Dumont, an elegant woman and a superior gambler, opened blackjack parlors in California and Nevada and followed gold rush booms. During the 1860s, after a short disastrous marriage, she chased strikes in Montana and Idaho, making only enough for drink and shelter. Financial failure, desire for revenge against her ex-husband, and aging coarsened her features and darkened the hair on her upper lip, giving her the nickname of "Madame Moustache."

• Gertrudis Barcelo ("La Tules") was the preeminent monte bank dealer and saloon keeper in New Mexico in the 1830s and 1840s. A capable, literate businesswoman and socialite, she was adored by all levels of New Mexican society. Most Americans, however, reviled her as evil, immoral, ugly, and brash, seemingly because she did not conform to their ideal of the genteel inferior housewife.

FARO

Faro, one of the oldest banking games, probably came from Italy. Giovanni Jacobo Casanova, who gambled at cards for a living, especially enjoyed playing faro. It is related historically to the games of lansquenet and monte bank. The name may have come from a pharaoh pictured on an early card. Faro was very popular in France during the reign of Louis XIV (1643-1715) and was brought to America by the French in New Orleans.

Faro was the most popular gambling game in America in the late nineteenth century. Wyatt Earp, a marshal in Dodge City, Kansas, dealt faro. He later was part-owner of a saloon in Tombstone, Arizona, and made more from gambling than from law enforcement.

Today faro is found only in a few Nevada casinos. Though a compli-cated system of combination betting exists, the simple game is described here.

Object of the game. To bet correctly on the face value of any card to win or lose.

Number of players. Any number.

Terms.
"Soda": The first card played on a deal. It does not participate in the play

"Loser": The second card played; in rounds after the first, it is the first card played

"Winner": The third card played; in rounds after the first, the second card played

Equipment. A table layout of one suit (customarily spades) and a standard deck of fifty-two cards. Suits have no rank; only face values are important. Players must have a method for keeping track of the values that have been played; pencil and paper work fine. Players also need markers to identify cards bet to lose (in the past, a copper token was used, hence, "coppering a bet").

The layout. A spade suit is laid out on the table:

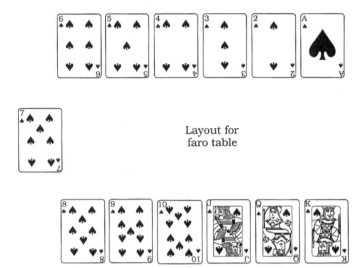

Layout for
faro table

Placing bets. Players can bet on any card value, either to win or lose when that number shows next. The bet is placed on the card on the table; if the bet is to lose, a marker is placed on the bet.

Playing faro. When all bets are placed, the banker (dealer) plays the first card (soda) and sets it aside. The next card dealt is a loser and the third, a winner. The bets on those two ranks are immediately settled at 1:1. Other bets are not affected and are left on the layout. Players may now bet on the next round.

The losing card begins a lose pile; the winning card, a win pile. When all bets are placed, another lose card and win card, in order, are turned up and bets settled. As play progresses, the players and the banker must keep track of all cards that have been played. A bet remaining when all the cards of that value have been played is a "sleeper," and the first person to grab it, keeps it.

On standard bets, the banker claims half of the bets when the winning and losing cards are both the same number.

After the forty-ninth card (a winner) has been dealt, there are three cards left. Players know the ranks of the cards (if they've been keeping good track of things!) and now bet on the order in which they will appear. The banker pays 4:1 for naming the correct order (odds are really 5:1 for the six possible orders, so the banker has an edge). If there is a pair ("cathop"), the banker pays 1:1 (the actual odds being 2:1, an edge for the banker). If there are three cards of the same rank, the betting is on color order and pays 2:1. Winning- and losing-card bets are not settled on the last three cards.

RED DOG

Object of the game. To hold a card in hand of higher rank (in the same suit) than one turned up from a stock pile.

Number of players. Any number from three to ten.

Equipment. A standard deck of fifty-two cards, ranking from A (high) to 2 (low).

Playing and betting. Each player, including the dealer, antes into the pool. The dealer deals five cards to each player (four to each with nine or ten players), one at a time. He places the remaining deck face down.

Beginning to the left of the dealer, each player looks at his hand. He may:

Pass, discarding his hand unshown to a "deadwood" pile and putting one chip into the pool

Bet any amount *up to* the value of the pool that he has a card of the same suit that will beat the top card face down on the deck. He states his bet and puts it by the pool

The dealer turns up the top card of the deck. If the bettor has one card that is higher in the same suit, he shows that card and the dealer pays him the amount of his stake from the pool. The deck card and the player's hand are discarded face down to the deadwood and the play moves to the next player.

If the player cannot beat the turned-up card, he exposes his hand to the players before discarding it. His stake is added to the pool, which increases the possible bet for the next player.

Subsequent players, in turn, bet or pass. The dealer turns up a new card for each player.

If one player wins all the chips from the pool, each player antes as before to form a new one. If the pool has dropped in amount at the completion of a round, the players each ante again. The deal then passes to the left.

Strategy. At the beginning of a deal, a player can assess his hand and know how many of the other forty-seven cards outside his hand he can beat and how many beat him. For example, an A beats any card of the same suit, a 10 beats eight lower cards while four beat the 10, and a void beats no cards in that suit. Initially, to make a safe bet, a player should have two high cards in two different suits. His advantage or disadvantage changes as play continues.

THE FARM

Two hundred years ago, a French book commented that a game called the farm was very old, "but was still played in the provinces." The farm was the basis for many other games, including blackjack and macao.

Object of the game. To reach a count of 16 or as near as possible without exceeding it.

Number of players. Any number, but best for six to twelve players.

Term.
"The farm": Pool of initial antes from each player

Equipment. Forty-five cards from a standard deck — all 8s are removed and all 6s except for the ♥6. Each A counts 1; court cards count 10; and other cards, their face value.

Playing and betting. Each player antes one chip to form the farm. Players then bid, in rotation, for the farm and the right to be the farmer (dealer/ banker). The highest bidder puts the amount of his bid into the farm, then shuffles and deals one card face down to the other players. He must be careful not to expose the bottom card of the pack.

Each player, in turn, must draw one card (and may draw more) to try to reach, but not exceed, 16. The cards are dealt by the dealer *from the bottom of the pack* and turned face up. If a player exceeds 16, he does not expose his hand until the end of play when he pays the *farmer* (not the farm) one chip for every point in his hand over 16.

Any player having exactly 16 wins the farm and all the chips. He takes the farm and becomes the next farmer.

If two or more players have 16, the one that has the ♥6 wins; if no player has the ♥6, the one with the fewest cards wins. If this is a tie, the hand nearest the dealer, counting from his left, wins. If no player has exactly 16, the pool and the farmer stay the same for the next deal, but the player having the closest to 16 is the winner and collects one chip from each player except the farmer.

Strategy. It is better to avoid loss rather than to risk a bust. It is dangerous to draw to a total of more than 9, but best to wait for a luckier hand.

MACAO

A game similar to the farm, macao became the French game of vingt-et-un, which was corrupted to van john in Britain, pontoon in Australia, and twenty-one (blackjack) in America. George Bryan Brummell (Beau Brummell) favored White's club in London, where he most often played macao. His fortunes came and went and he died a pauper in a madhouse.

Object of the game. To reach a count of 9 with one or more cards.

Number of players. Any number.

Term.
"Natural": The deal of a 9, 8, or 7 on the first round

Equipment. A standard deck of fifty-two cards. Court cards and 10s all count 0, 9s through 2s count their face value, and As (low) count 1.

Playing and betting. Each player places a bet, then the dealer deals one card face down to each player and himself. Naturals are turned up immediately and the bets settled. If the dealer has a natural, he collects the bets from players with a numerically lower natural or no natural.

If the dealer has no natural, when bets of those numbers are settled, the remaining players in turn may draw one or more cards to try to reach 9 or close to it without exceeding it. The dealer also has the opportunity to draw to his hand. When a player ties the dealer, no bet is paid.

Settling the bets. A player is paid 3:1 for a natural 9, 2:1 for a natural 8, and 1:1 for a natural 7 except that dealer ties a 9 with a 9, beats an 8 with a 9, beats a 7 with an 8 or 9, and ties with the same number. Dealer pays 1:1 for hands beating his that have more than one card and collects the bets of players with lower hands.

ALL FOURS (SEVEN-UP)

In 1674, Charles Cotton described all fours as a very popular English game. Brought by the colonists to America, it was commonly played for a hundred years, until gradually it was replaced by poker as the favorite gambling game. Bret Harte, O. Henry, Mark Twain, and other storytellers mention all fours.

The game is known by several names: all fours (for the four ways to score points), seven-up (for the 7 points to win), old sledge, and high-low-jack. All fours preceded many modern games, such as cinch and auction pitch.

Though historically a gambling game, there appear to be no set rules for betting. Several possibilities are evident, however. All players may ante and the first to reach game takes the chips. Or chips may be awarded for each of the four points with a larger award given for game. Or you may be creative – you're on your own!

Object of the game. To hold the highest and lowest trumps in hand, to turn up the J for trumps or take the J trump in a trick, and to take cards that count toward game.

Number of players. Two or three may play as individuals or four in partnerships of two each.

Terms.

"Running the cards": Dealing another round of three cards and turning up a new trump

"Eldest hand": Dealer's opponent if two play; hand to the left of the dealer if more than two play

"Stand": To accept the turn-up as trump

"Beg": To reject the turn-up as trump

Equipment. A standard deck of fifty-two cards, ranking from A (high) to 2 (low).

Dealing the hands. After the cards are shuffled and cut, the dealer gives six cards (three at a time) to each player, starting on his left. The dealer turns up the next card for trump; if he turns up a J, he immediately scores 1 point. When more than two play, only the dealer and the eldest hand may look at their cards until the first trump is accepted or rejected.

Eldest hand looks at his cards and may stand or beg. If he stands, accepting the trump, all players pick up their hands and play begins. If he begs, the dealer may give him 1 point ("gift") to let the trump stand or "refuse gift" and deal three more cards to each player and turn up a new trump. Dealer must refuse gift if eldest hand is only 1 point short of game.

If the new trump is the same suit as before, the cards are run again until a different suit is turned up. Dealer cannot score for a later turn-up of a J in the rejected suit. The last card of the deck cannot be turned up as trump. If the whole deck is run without a new suit being turned, the cards are collected, shuffled, cut, and dealt again by the same dealer.

But if the second turn-up is a different suit than the first, it fixes trump and play begins.

Playing all fours. If the pack has been run, players discard enough cards to reduce their hands to six. The eldest hand then leads any card. If a player is able to follow suit, he must do so; if unable to follow suit, he may trump or discard.

The trick is won by the highest trump (if there is a trump) or by the highest card of the suit led. The winner of a trick leads to the next trick. When play is completed, players examine the cards in the tricks they have taken and count their points.

Scoring. A total of 4 points may be scored:

High – highest trump in play; scores 1 point for the player to whom it was dealt

Low – lowest trump in play; scores 1 point for the player to whom it was dealt (in some versions, it is 1 point for the player who takes it in play)

Jack – J of trumps; 1 point for dealer if turned up for trump; otherwise, 1 point for the player who takes it in a trick

Game – highest total of points for cards won in play; scores 1 point for player with highest total. Only As, Ks, Qs, Js, and 10s are counted; 9s and below have no value. Point values for counters are as follows:

Each A	4 points
Each K	3 points
Each Q	2 points
Each J	1 point
Each 10	10 points

With two or four players, the side with the highest total points wins 1 point for game; if there is a tie, the nondealer (or nondealer's side) scores the point. In a three-handed game, the player with the highest total scores 1 point. If dealer ties with one opponent, the opponent wins; if two non-dealers tie, game point is not scored.

Points are always scored in the order given. If both players (or sides) score enough to win in a single hand, the points are scored in the order given (high, low, jack, game) to determine the winner. The J will not always be in play, but the other three points are scored. If there is only one trump in play, it scores as both high and low. The first player to reach a total of 7 points wins the game. If a dealer needs only 1 point to reach 7 and he turns the J, he wins without playing out the hand. After each hand, the deal passes to the left.

VARIATIONS OF ALL FOURS

California jack. In this variation for two players, the trump is established by cutting the deck before the deal. After the six cards are given to each player, the pile is faced up. The nondealer leads. The winner of the first trick takes the top card from the pile; the other player, the next card. The hands are thus restored to six cards after each trick. When the pile is gone, the last cards are played out.

Play completed, each player examines the cards in his tricks. The 4 points are scored for *high* (the A of trump), *low* (the 2 of trump), *jack* (the J of trump), and *game* (points counted as in all fours). The game can be 7 or 10 points. Like all fours, points are scored in the given order to determine the winner.

Shasta sam. In this variation of california jack, the pile stays face down. This eliminates keeping track of what has been drawn and forcing an opponent to win the trick when it is desirable (such as when the top card of the pile is a non-counter of 9 or below).

BRAG (TRADITIONAL)

Brag is thought to have originated from an old Spanish game called primero. Following several generations of related games in France, it emerged as brag in England during the Tudor reign (1485-1603). Brag has the element of bluffing and, with other games that provided new conventions, it is an ancestor of modern-day poker.

Object of the game. To outlast the betting and win the bets of the other players.

Number of players. From three to twelve, usually from five to eight. One is chosen dealer; after each hand the deal passes to the left.

Term.
"Braggers": Any of the three wild cards: ♦A, ♦9, and ♣J, which are of equal rank. They can hold any value a player wishes, but are not considered wild when they represent their own face values

Equipment. A standard deck of fifty-two cards. Their rank is from A (high) to 2 (low).

Dealing the hands. When the cards have been shuffled and cut, the dealer puts an ante in the center of the table and deals three cards to each player.

Evaluating the hands. Straights and flushes are ignored. Only three of a kind, pairs, and high cards are considered. The ranking of hands is listed (from highest to lowest) and illustrated below.

Pair royale. Three cards of equal rank, e.g., three 2s. A pair royale without a bragger is higher than a pair royale with a bragger. When more than one hand has a pair royale, the face value determines the higher hand.

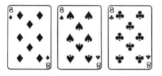

Natural pair royale

Pair royale with bragger

Pair. The next highest hand is a pair. A natural pair is higher than one with a bragger. The rank of the unpaired cards decides the higher hand when the pairs are the same.

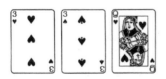

Natural pair

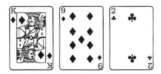

Pair with bragger

High card. Hands without a pair are decided on their number value. If the two high cards are equal, the value of the second card decides; if those are also equal, then the third card determines the winning hand.

High card

Betting. Each player, in turn rotating left, looks at his cards. He may drop out, place a bet equal to the dealer's ante, or raise the bet (as in poker). If he raises, the players following must match his bet or drop out. Players who have already bet must bring their bets up to the new level (or raise) on their next turn or drop out, forfeiting their bets.

The betting is completed when all but one player has dropped out (he may take all bets without showing his hand) or when all players remaining have bet equal amounts. In this case, no player may raise again and players show their hands. The player with the best hand takes in the pool. If two hands are equal, the two players share the pool.

VARIATION OF BRAG

Three-stake brag. Three-stake brag is an old variation. Before the deal, three pools are made by three equal antes from each player. The dealer deals two cards to each player face down, then a third face up.

The winner of the first stake is the player with the highest card face up (braggers count their natural value). If two or more players have equal cards, the player closest to the dealer's left wins the first bet.

The second stake is won the same way as regular brag. Players look at their hands and bet — a raise or a match — or drop out. If no one bets, the best hand wins.

The third stake is won at the end of the hand. The players show their cards and add up the total count: Ks, Qs, and Js count 10, As count 11, and the others count their face value. The closest player to 31 (over or under) wins the round. However, any player under 31, beginning on the dealer's left, may draw from the pack until he decides to stop. If he goes over 31 from the draws, he is bust and cannot win. Should two or more remaining players be the same distance from 31, the player nearest the dealer's left wins the round.

MONTE BANK

Monte bank is a simple gambling game whose early roots can be traced back to the same ones as poker (which is relatively modern – within the last 150 years). It is a favorite Spanish and Spanish-American game.

Object of the game: To correctly bet on whether a card of one suit will turn up before another.

Number of players. Any number.

Terms.

"Bottom layout": The two cards from the bottom of the deck placed face up on the table

"Top layout": The two cards from the top of the deck placed face up on the table

"Gate": The card exposed on the bottom of the deck when it is turned over

Equipment. Forty cards – a standard fifty-two-card pack with the 8s, 9s, and 10s removed.

Setting the bets: A banker is chosen; he may pass the bank after five hands or remain banker for the duration of the game. After the deck is shuffled and cut, the banker draws two cards from the bottom of the deck for the bottom layout and two cards from the top for the top layout.

Players place their bets on whichever layout they choose. The banker then turns the pack face up to expose the gate card.

Paying the bets. If the gate is the same suit as either card in the top or bottom layout, the banker pays the bets on that layout at 1:1. If both, he pays both. If a layout does not have a card of the same suit as the gate, the banker collects the bets on it. If a layout contains two cards of the same suit, the bettors on that layout collect 3:1 if they win.

There is a slight advantage for the banker unless there is one card of each suit in the two layouts.

After all bets are settled, the layout and gate cards are discarded. Two new layouts and a new gate card are created. Play continues as before until the deck has been run, then it is reshuffled.

Top layout

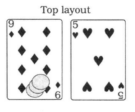

Bottom layout

Gate

Bets on both layouts win; had the gate card been a club or diamond only those on one layout would win

LANSQUENET

Lansquenet is a German game named for Landsknecht (foot soldier). It is believed that German soldiers introduced it to the French during the Franco-Prussian War (1870-1871).

Object of the game. To bet correctly that a card of one value will turn up before another.

Number of players. Any number. One is chosen banker, which passes to the left after each deal.

Term.
"Hand cards": the first two cards of different face values turned up before the deal begins. No bets are made on hand cards

Equipment. A standard deck of fifty-two cards. Suits have no rank; only face values are important.

Placing bets. When the deck has been shuffled and cut, the banker deals the top two cards face up in a row on the table (hand cards). He deals one card face up to himself ("banker's card") and one for the group of players ("players' card"). If either the banker's card or the players' card matches a hand card, it is placed on it and another card dealt.

The players place their bets on the players' card, each stating the amount of his bet. They are betting that a card matching the banker's card will turn up before a card matching the players' card.

The banker draws cards one at a time from the top of the pack and turns them face up:

Match for a players' card. Banker wins the bets on that card; the pair of matching cards is placed beside the banker's card to separate it from cards still in play.

Match for banker's card. Banker pays all players for their bets at 1:1 and his deal ends.

Match for neither card. The card becomes another players' card and they may bet on it. A player may not bet on another card in the same deal except at the same stake.

Match for either of the hand cards. The card is placed on the card it matches. If both hand cards are matched before either the players' first card or the banker's card is matched, the banker wins all bets, collects the cards, and deals again.

Strategy. The odds of lansquenet are the same for both player and banker; initially when a bet is placed, three cards of the rank of the banker's card and three of the players' card are still in the deck.

Players' cards

1st   2nd   3rd

Hand cards    Banker's card

The hand cards, banker's card,
and players' cards with bets in place

NAPOLEON

Napoleon descended from the early game of triomphe, which "fathered" the large family of euchre games. Some (ecarte in France, spoil five in Ireland, napoleon in England, euchre in America) have been considered as national games at one time and have survived; others of the euchre family have become obsolete.

Object of the game. To bid and make the number of tricks specified in the bid.

Number of players. Two to six, four is best.

Terms.
"Nap": A bid to take all five tricks

"Declarer": The player winning the bid

Equipment. A standard fifty-two-card deck. The cards rank from A (high) to 2 (low).

Dealing and bidding. The dealer deals five cards, one at a time face down, to each player. Each player, starting to the left of the dealer, may pass or may bid the number of tricks (two or more) he thinks he can take given the right to name trump. If he bids, he does not yet name the trump suit. Each following bid must be higher than the preceding bid: two (first bid), three, four, or nap (five). If no one bids, the dealer must bid at least one (the only time a bid of "one" is allowed).

The declarer then leads the first card, which sets the trump suit. On all leads, each player must follow suit if he can; if he cannot, he may trump or discard. The highest card of the suit led takes the trick or, if trumped, the highest trump. The winner of each trick leads to the next. Tricks taken are placed face down, but separated for easy counting. They may not be reexamined. As soon as the declarer gets the number of tricks he has bid, the hand is abandoned (overtricks have no value); the declarer wins chips from each player according to the payment schedule. If he fails to make his bid, he is penalized and pays each player according to the schedule.

Settling the bid. The payment schedule is shown below:

Bid:	Declarer wins:	Declarer pays:
One	1 chip	1 chip
Two	2 chips	2 chips
Three	3 chips	3 chips
Four	4 chips	4 chips
Nap	10 chips	5 chips

Strategy. With four or five players, the majority of the cards remain in the pack. With three trumps, including the A and K and an outside A, a player should make at least three tricks and probably four. With four small trumps, even with an outside A, the odds favor making only three tricks.

During play, a player should try to take every trick he can. It is rarely profitable to withhold a card that can top a previous card.

SOME VARIATIONS OF NAPOLEON

Misery. Misery — a contract to lose all tricks in a game with no trump — is a bid ranking between the bids of three and four, and three chips are won from or lost to each player.

Wellington. Wellington is a bid only made above nap. It is a contract to win all five tricks at double the stakes (declarer wins 20 and loses 10).

Blucher. Blucher is a bid made over wellington and pays or loses triple stakes over nap (declarer wins 30 and loses 15).

Peep. Peep allows the declarer who has bid nap to change a card in his hand for the top card of the pack if he wishes. Other players may ante one chip into a pool and look at the top card before the declarer exchanges his card. The pool is taken by the declarer if he makes his bid; if he fails, it is picked up by the next player to successfully win a bid.

Purchase nap. Purchase nap lets any player look at the top card of the pack before bidding by putting one chip into the pool. The player who becomes declarer, if he has paid to look at the top card, can change it for one in his hand before he leads.

POPE JOAN

Pope joan is a very old gambling game based on two earlier games. The first — cometé — developed in France and has been related to apprehension over the coming of Halley's comet in 1682. Suits were played upward in sequence like the tail of a comet; a face-down card stopping the running of a sequence was analogous to the fear that the world would stop when the comet came. Imported to England, the name was corrupted to commit. The second — matrimony — contributed to pope joan the paired face-card combinations, which satirized the behavior of the royalty.

Object of the game. To play cards that allow collecting chips from the eight pools and to be the first player to get rid of all the cards in hand.

Number of players. Any number from three to eight, but four or more is best.

Terms.
"Confederacy": The K and J of trumps played from the same hand. This combination is seldom made part of the game, but if it is an additional pool is provided for it

"Pope joan": The ♦9

"Stop hand": The extra hand between the dealer and the player to his immediate right

"Stop card": A card for which there is no next-higher card in the same suit available for playing. Stop cards include:

All Ks (highest card in each suit)
♦7 (the ♦8 is removed from the deck)
Any card one number below a card in the stop hand
Any card one number below cards already played (e.g., if ♠6, ♠7, ♠8, and ♠9 have been run in sequence previously, the ♠5 is a stop card)

"Trump": The suit of the last card turned up

Equipment. A fifty-one-card pack; the ♦8 is omitted. The remaining cards rank from A (low) through K (high). Players also need a number of counters (poker chips, pennies, etc.), all having equal value.

In the early days, pope joan was played on elaborately decorated circular tables with compartments to contain the bets. You can make your own board or use something as simple as sign markers to identify the placement of the eight pools:

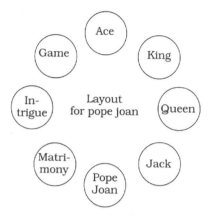

Layout for pope joan

Dealing the cards. The cards are cut for deal; the lowest card identifies the dealer. Each player contributes a counter to each of the eight (or nine, with confederacy) pools.

The dealer passes out the entire deck, one card at a time, beginning on his left. He deals out a card to the stop hand just before he deals his own card each round. If there are not enough cards to complete a round, the dealer may put all cards except the last into the stop hand or deal around to the left until the last card is reached. The last card is faced up for trump and placed on the stop hand; it belongs to the dealer.

If A, K, Q, or J is turned up, the dealer takes the counters on that marker. If pope joan is turned up, he takes all the counters on the eight markers; the game is over and the deal passes to the left (with some players, turning ♦9 only gives the dealer the counters on that marker − you decide).

Playing pope joan. The player on the dealer's left leads any card, plays it in front of him, and names its suit and value. He may continue to play one or more following cards in the same suit in upward sequence, naming them, until he cannot play again. Then any player who can continue the sequence plays his card(s) to his own pile and names them. The play proceeds thusly until a stop card is reached. When a stop occurs, all played cards are turned face down and the player of the stop card leads to the next sequence.

Any player who plays the K, Q, J, or A of trumps or pope joan takes the chips on those pools immediately. If a player plays both the trump Q and K, he takes any chips on Q, on K, and on matrimony. If he plays both the trump J and Q, he takes any chips on J, on Q, and on intrigue. The cards must actually be played to collect the chips. However, if the dealer has turned up the K, Q, or J for trump, that card is considered to be already played by the dealer; if he later plays the second court card in the trump suit, he may take any chips for that card as well as the matrimony or intrigue chips for the combination.

If confederacy has been made part of the game (there is a pool for it) and one player plays the trump J and K, he takes any chips in J, K, and confederacy, but he must pay a penalty of one counter to the pope joan pool.

In some localities, the playing of the ♦9 constitutes a universal stop, its holder immediately wins the game, and a new deal follows. Usually, however, pope joan ends the deal only when it is turned up as trump.

Any chips not collected during a hand remain in their respective pools for collection with new chips on a subsequent hand.

Settling the bets. When one player has rid himself of all his cards, he wins the game. He immediately gets all the counters on the game marker. Additionally, from each of the other players, he gets one counter for each card left in their respective hands, except that a player still holding ♦9 pays nothing.

One other variation is the pope joan hand. To end the session, all counters in the pool are placed in a pile in the center and each player antes one counter to increase the pile. The cards are dealt one at a time left to right face up. The player who gets the pope joan card takes the final pool.

A VARIATION OF POPE JOAN

Newmarket. Newmarket is a more modern and simplified version of pope joan. There are a number of similar games with names such as boodle, stops, michigan, chicago, and saratoga; rules among these games differ slightly.

Any number of players from three to eight may play. The fifty-one-card pack is used, cards ranking from 2 (low) to A (high). The layout consists of a pool and four "boodle" cards — A, K, Q, J of differing suits from another pack (in some places these are specified as ♥A, ♦K, ♠Q, and ♣J).

Players decide who will deal first. The dealer has an advantage because he may exchange his hand for the extra hand, so players must deal an equal number of

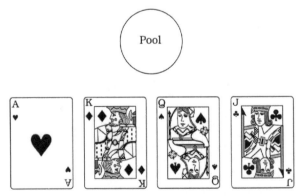

The four boodle cards and the pool

times. Each player places one chip on each card and one in the pool.

The dealer deals the pack, one at a time, including the extra hand between himself and the first player to his *left*. The dealer, after looking at his hand, may swap it for the extra hand (but cannot change it back). The unused hand stays faced down on the table for the remainder of the game.

The player on the dealer's left leads any suit, but the card must be the lowest card of that suit in his hand. He names the card, placing it in front of him. The player with the next highest card in that suit plays it and names its rank, and so forth until the suit is stopped either by an A or by a card being unavailable because it is in the unused hand. The player who played the last card before the suit was stopped leads a new suit by leading his lowest card in a suit and naming its rank and suit. If the only cards he holds are in the suit that has just been stopped, he must pass the lead to the player on his left.

Any time a player plays a duplicate of a boodle card, he takes the counters on that card. Any chips remaining at the end of the game stay on the boodle card to be won on a future deal.

Play ends when one player is out of cards. He wins the counters on the pool.

If a player is found to have played a card other than his lowest in a suit, he must replace any counters won on boodle cards and pay each of the other players one counter as a penalty. If a player did not play a card when he was able to (causing a false stop), he must replace any counters won from boodle cards or the pool on that deal; if his misplay has stopped another player from playing the boodle card in that suit, the erring player must pay him the number of counters on that card.

THREE-CARD MONTE

The history of three-card monte is unknown, but its popularity in stories about the Old West requires that it be included in this book.

Basically the same as the shell game, several rogues made their fortunes playing three-card monte. For instance, George H. Devol could cheat skillfully at cards by age seventeen; he swindled soldiers on the Rio Grande during the Mexican War. But his heyday was on the Mississippi where he played poker and three-card monte.

Elijah ("Brother") Skaggs got his sobriquet because he looked and dressed like a traveling parson. His most successful scheme came in New Orleans after 1830. There he schooled handsome young men in how to cheat, then he staked their efforts and gave them twenty-five percent of the profits. His system did well for twenty years and spread faro and three-card monte to many areas.

Object of the game. To identify the black card.

Number of players. Any number and a banker.

Equipment. Three cards, two red and one black. Traditionally they are the red As and the ♠A. The cards are often curved slightly lengthwise so they can be picked up easily.

Playing and betting. The banker shows the black card to the other players, then lays the cards face down on a table. He moves the cards around rapidly, the movements designed to confuse the players as to the location of the black card. When the cards come to rest, the players bet as to which one is the ♠A. If the banker pays 1:1, he wins on average; paying 2:1 evens the odds.

HAZARD

Hazard, a dice game, was played as early as the fourteenth century; betting odds were not set. It became very popular in the eighteenth century and was often enjoyed at exclusive gambling clubs, such as Brook's and Arthur's. It is said that Beau Brummel, playing at Brook's, once won a fortune by beating a brewer twenty-five times in a row; he then swore to "never drink any porter" again other than the brewer's! In 1887, Edmund Hoyle published odds for the thirty-six combinations possible for the roll of two dice and betting changed to reflect the standardized odds.

Modern hazard, a very different game from the early version, can still be found in a few casinos. Three dice are used instead of two, more bets (such as "odd" or "even," "high" or "low") are possible, and winning payments are set. Generally, hazard has been surpassed today by craps.

One basic adaptation of the early game is presented here.

Object of the game. To bet correctly on the rolls of two dice.

Number of players. Any number.

Terms.
"Caster": The player rolling the dice

"Chance": The first roll of the dice (after the main is set) that is neither a winning or losing roll when compared to the main

"Main": A number from 5 to 9, inclusive. Some rules say that the player merely states the number to set main. By other rules, the player rolls the dice to set main; if he does not get a number from 5 through 9, he must pass the dice to the left

Equipment. A table and two dice.

Playing hazard. Once the main is set, the other players bet and the caster rolls the dice again (the chance roll). There may be three outcomes, two of which are immediately the caster's win or loss:

If main is	Caster wins if dice total:	Caster loses if dice total:	Caster neither wins nor loses if dice total:
5	5	2, 3, 11, or 12	4, 6, 7, 8, 9, or 10
6	6 or 12	2, 3, or 11	4, 5, 7, 8, 9 or 10
7	7 or 11	2, 3, or 12	4, 5, 6, 8, 9, or 10
8	8 or 12	2, 3, or 11	4, 5, 6, 7, 9, or 10
9	9	2, 3, 11, or 12	4, 5, 6, 7, 8, or 10

Bettors may change their bets between any subsequent rolls.

If caster does not win or lose on the chance roll, he continues rolling until the dice reflect either the main or the chance total. If he rolls main, he now *loses* and must pay all bettors the amount of their stakes and pass the dice to the left. If he rolls the chance total, he collects all bets, keeps the dice, and the game begins again.

Indian Games

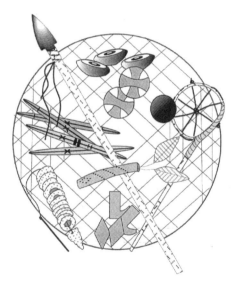

INDIAN GAMES

In his classic book, *Games of the North American Indians,* Stewart Culin divides American Indian games into two general types: games of chance and games of dexterity. Games of pure skill and calculation, such as chess, appear to be absent from Native American pastimes.

Both chance and dexterity games are found in all tribes and there appear to be commonalities between their games, even when the tribes are geographically disparate and linguistically unrelated. Most differences are in the materials used in play — factors governed by what is available in the environment — rather than the object of a game or its rules. Some older games may have begun in the southwestern United States and been progressively modified as they moved north and east.

Many Indian games appear to relate to origin myths. The actions are analagous to a series of contests in which First-man overcame an enemy of the human race by cunning, skill, and luck. Common to many tribes is the concept of the divine twins, who played with and contended against each other. The twins' games were adapted to play by humans; gaming implements, such as stick dice, were modifications of the twins' symbols and weapons (war clubs, arrows, shields, etc.).

Frequently Indian games were the purview of adults and older youth. They often were played seasonally, their enjoyment being a component of festivals and religious celebrations to please the gods — to bring rain, to encourage fertility or long life, to cure sickness, to expel demons. Gaming implements were things to please the gods and were among the objects sacrificed on ceremonial altars.

Indian children seldom competed in organized activities that had formal rules and competitive outcomes. Instead, they played informally: mock fighting, spinning tops, etc. American Indians apparently saw no need to use games to school their children in life skills at a very young age as did Europeans. In fact, most Native American pastimes were little impacted by interaction with Europeans. The Indians did borrow a few games from their conquerors, such as nine men's morris and the use of playing cards. The English and Spanish adopted games liberally from the Indians, however, often giving the contests new names and identities.

GAMES OF CHANCE (DICE GAMES)

The most common games of chance, usually played silently, involved some type of throwing pieces much like European dice. Materials were split cane; wood blocks; wood or bone staves; animal teeth; shells; fruit pits; grains of corn; discs of bone, shell, brass, or clay. The items were shaped and colored with distinguishing markings. The "dice" could be thrown by hand or tossed in a basket (more common in women's games). The object of the games was to throw the dice in combinations that accumulated enough points to win. Native Americans were avid gamblers; heavy betting often occurred and high stakes were wagered. Five dice-type games are presented here: a widespread game called hubbub and games from the Cree, Gros Ventre, Seneca, and Passamaquoddy.

HUBBUB

The name "hubbub" came from a New England writer, William Wood, who described the game in 1634. Hubbub was played by both eastern and western tribes. Though mostly a women's game in the West, men in the East played it with an accompanying song.

Object of the game. To throw the dice in certain combinations to accumulate enough points to win.

Number of players. Two or more.

Equipment. Five dice made of bone or plum pits. Two were alike in shape and markings (here, round), three were marked alike, but could be different in shape (here, oblong). Markings were only on one side, the other being blank. Players also used a small basket (6-8 inches across) for tossing the dice. They kept score with sticks.

Round dice
(marked side)

Oblong dice
(marked side)

Playing hubbub. The first player throws the dice up, letting them fall back into the basket. So long as she continues to score, her turn continues. Once she has no score for a toss, the basket and dice pass to the next player.

Scoring. Scoring combinations are as follows:

Marked side of one only of either round or oblong	0 points (basket passes)
Two round dice with marked side up (oblongs either marked or blank)	3 points
Three oblong dice marked side up (rounds blank)	3 points
Two round dice with marked side up (oblongs blank)	3 points
Four dice with marked side up (oblong or round)	1 point

Five blank dice (oblong and round)	1 point
Five dice with marked side up (oblong and round)	8 points

The game is won by the first player to collect sticks totaling 100 points.

CREE DICE GAME

Both men and women joined in playing this game.

Object of the game. To throw the dice in combinations that score points.

Number of players. Any number of players, individually or as partners.

Equipment. Eight dice about 3/4 inch long: four are shaped as hooks, the other four as diamonds. Each die has a light side and a dark side. A wooden bowl, originally shaped like a tin pan and about 8 1/2 inches in diameter, is used to shake the dice.

Diamonds
(light and dark)

Hooks
(light and dark)

Playing the Cree game. The dice are placed in the bowl, which is held in both hands. The bowl then is moved sharply and quickly downward to shake the dice. Only the up faces of the dice score:

All light sides up	100 points
All dark sides up	80 points
Seven light sides, one dark side up	30 points
All four hooks and one diamond with light sides up	10 points
All four hooks and one diamond with dark sides up	8 points
All four diamonds and one hook with light sides up	6 points
All four diamonds and one hook with dark sides up	4 points
Each hook-shaped piece on edge	2 points

The game is won by the first player (or partnership) to reach 100 points.

GROS VENTRE DICE GAME

Object of the game. To throw the sticks in point-winning combinations.

Number of players. Two.

Equipment. Four oblong wooden sticks about 10 1/2 inches in length. Two of the sticks are identical, painted green on both sides with red lines painted in the cut-out decoration on one side. The other two sticks are painted red (both sides) with green in the lines on the marked side, but they are not identical; one has two buckskin thongs wrapped around it. There are twelve counting sticks, ten peeled and two with the bark left on.

Two green sticks	Two red sticks
(marked sides)	(marked sides, one
	with two bands)

Playing the Gros Ventre dice game. The sticks are thrown from the hand to the ground so they land on their ends and fall over. Score accumulates as follows:

Plain side of banded stick, marked side of three others	6 points
Marked side of banded stick and plain side of three others	6 points
All marked sides up	4 points
All plain sides up	4 points
Two marked sides up (within pair)	2 points
Two plain sides up (within pair)	2 points

The score is kept with the counting sticks (you decide their values) until one player wins all of them.

SENECA DICE GAME

Object of the game. To throw the dice in combinations that win points.

Number of players. Originally, this game was played by two players in public, the loser giving his position to the next player at the termination of a game. In intimate groups, more players were included.

Equipment. Original dice were eight elk horn slices, each rounded and polished and slightly burned on one side to make it darker. In addition, a pile of perhaps fifty beans were used as counters.

One of four
light dice

One of four
dark dice

Playing the Seneca dice game. The players spread a blanket and sit down on it. The first player shakes the dice in his hands and throws them onto the blanket. As long as he scores, he continues to throw the dice. The other player takes his turn when the first player fails to score, and so on. Scoring is as follows:

Less than six dice of the same color	0 points (dice pass)
Six dice of the same color	2 points
Seven dice of the same color	4 points
Eight dice of the same color	20 points

To keep score, the player winning points takes an equal number of beans from the pile. When the pile is depleted, the winner collects beans from his opponent's pile. If more than two play, each individual pays the winner the proper amount of beans, even if players are partners. That is, if all sticks are turned up one color, the winning player collects 20 beans from the pile. If the pile is exhausted, however, the winner collects 20 beans from each of the other players.

The winner is the player who collects all the beans.

PASSAMAQUODDY DICE GAME

This game is representative of a number of similar games. Primarily it is a game of chance, but skill in tossing the dice may be helpful in achieving a successful outcome.

Object of the game. To toss the dice in point-winning combinations.

Number of players. Two, usually women.

Equipment. Six thin dice (bone, plum pits, etc.) with a carved or colored design on one side (blank on the other). Players also need a shallow bowl or dish for tossing the dice. Score is kept with forty-eight small sticks and five large sticks, one of which is notched.

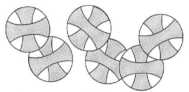

Decorated plum pit dice   Passamaquoddy bone dice

Playing the Passamaquoddy dice game. The players kneel facing each other. Counting sticks are placed in a pile accessible to both. The bowl with the dice is set on a cushion between the players.

The players take turns slapping the bowl down on the cushion with enough force to make the dice jump into the air and return to the bowl. If a player scores, she continues with another turn; if she fails to score, the bowl passes to her opponent. If a die jumps from the bowl, she must pass the bowl.

The game has two phases, unless Phase 1 ends in a tie.

Phase 1. Small counting sticks are taken first, then large ones. The notched stick, equal to three small sticks, is always picked up last. Scoring (simplified) is as follows:

Dice arrangement in bowl:	Sticks taken from pile:
Five dice same way up (marked or plain):	
First toss	Three small sticks
Second successive toss	Another nine small sticks
Third successive toss	Twelve small sticks or one big stick
Six dice same way up (marked or plain):	
First toss	Twelve small sticks or one big stick
Second successive toss	Thirty-six small sticks or three big sticks
Third successive toss	One big stick stood on end to show a debt of sixteen small sticks

The notched stick is the last one to be taken. If Phase 1 is a tie, the game is over; if Phase 1 is not a tie, Phase 2 begins.

Phase 2. Phase 2 is played like Phase 1. The sticks are valued differently, however, and sticks won are taken from the opponent, not from the pile. Sticks are paid thusly:

Dice arrangement in bowl:	Sticks taken from opponent:
Five dice same way up (marked or plain):	
First toss	Four small sticks
Second successive toss	Twelve small sticks
Third successive toss	Sixteen small sticks or one big stick
Six dice same way up (marked or plain):	
First toss	Sixteen small sticks or one big stick
Second successive toss	Forty-eight small sticks or three big sticks

When a player has no sticks left, she has lost the game.

GAMES OF CHANCE (GUESSING GAMES)

Guessing games are the second type of chance games. The object of all guessing games was for one player (or team) to hide a distinctive object so as to confuse an opponent whose task was to locate the object. Four types of guessing games were common: stick games, hand games, four-stick games, and hidden ball (moccasin) games.

In stick games, one person hides a distinctive shaft or disc among a number of other pieces. The pieces, divided into two groups, are held in hand or hidden in another material, such as a leather bag or a pile of bark. Three stick games are included here (Chippewa, Cree, Ataakut).

For hand games, the pieces are held in hand. Many materials were used—bones, notched sticks, small strings of beads—and sets were made in one or two pairs, one of the set being distinguished from the others in some way. Hand games were very common and crossed many linguistic families and localities. Perhaps their popularity was due, at least in part, to the fact that the games were played entirely with gestures, making play across tribes easier because they could rely on sign language. Often players sang and swayed while hiding the marked piece. Both men and women participated, though not together, and the number of players could vary from two to any number. The book includes two hand games, one from the Blackfeet and one from the Pima.

Four-stick games were played by a limited number of tribes, primarily those in the northern half of the western United States. The Klamath game is a four-stick game.

Moccasin games consist of one player hiding a distinctive object in one of several places. Original hiding places were often moccasins, but cane tubes or cups and other containers were used also. The hidden object could be a stick, bean, stone, ball, bullet or any similar small item. Moccasin games were played by men from Algonquin tribes, the Dakota, and some southwest tribes. This book includes two moccasin-type games—one is Chippewa, the other Walapai.

CHIPPEWA STICK GAME

Object of the game. To hide or to guess correctly which hand holds the odd stick.

Number of players. Two men.

Equipment. Eleven sticks about 18 inches in length.

Playing the Chippewa stick game. One player takes the sticks in his hands, five sticks in one hand, six in the other hand. His opponent indicates the hand he thinks has the extra stick. The motions of both players must be done very quickly. If the guesser is correct, he wins the wagers and takes the sticks; if he is incorrect, he loses the wagers and the holder arranges the sticks again.

CREE STICK GAME

The Cree game is played by men and/or women.

Object of the game. To hide or guess which of two stick bundles has an even number.

Number of players. Any number; players are divided into two teams, the members of which sit in lines opposite each other.

Equipment. Twenty-five sticks or slender willow withes.

Playing the Cree stick game. The first player secretly divides the sticks into two bundles, holding one in either hand. His opponent in the line opposite chooses the bundle that he believes has the even number of sticks. If the chooser is correct he wins; if he chooses the bundle with the odd number of sticks, he loses and the holding of the sticks passes to the next player along the holder's line.

ATAAKUT STICK GAME

Play of the game is accompanied by singers and a drummer.

Object of the game. To hide or guess which bundle of sticks has the banded stick.

Number of players. Two, who are called "leaders." Any number may participate by betting on the outcome.

Equipment. A set of thirty-one sticks, each about 8 1/2 inches long. One stick has a band of black paint near the middle.

Playing the Ataakut game. The leaders sit opposite each other on a blanket. One takes the sticks, holds them behind his back, and shuffles them around. He brings two bundles to the front with his arms extended and the sticks held so players cannot see the centers. The other leader points to the bundle he thinks holds the stick with the black band. If he is correct, he holds the bundles for the next rounds until his opponent can win them back. For each wrong guess, a penalty is paid; a penalty is also paid by the leader when he loses the deal.

BLACKFEET HAND GAME

This game is much like the European game of "button, button, who's got the button?" Wagers were made between facing opponents.

Object of the game. To hide or locate the marked bone.

Number of players. Two to twelve, divided into two teams in lines sitting opposite each other.

Equipment. Two small oblong bones, one with a black ring around it.

Playing the Blackfeet hand game. One player takes the bones and manipulates them between his moving hands. He may sway his arms and body and make many intricate movements to confuse his opponents. When he stops, his facing opponent tries to guess which hand has the banded bone. If the guesser is correct, he scores 1 point, otherwise the holder gets 1 point. The score is kept by sticks and the first team to reach 10 points wins the wagers.

PIMA HAND GAME

Object of the game. To hide or locate a small object among team members.

Number of players. Any number in teams with two chosen as leaders. Teams line up in two facing lines.

Equipment. A small object, usually a pottery shard. A line is drawn about 50 yards from one end of the two lines of players.

Playing the Pima hand game. One of the leaders carries the shard along behind his team and places it in the hands of one of his teammates. The opposite leader guesses who holds the shard. If he is wrong, the man farthest from the goal on the holding team runs to the front of the line and jumps over the leg of the first man in his line. This advances the line the width of one man and a jump toward the goal. If the leader's guess is correct, he gets the shard and play by the other team resumes as before. There is no advancment until a guess is missed.

KLAMATH FOUR-STICK GAME

Object of the game. To confuse an opponent or guess correctly the arrangement of four sticks.

Number of players. Two.

Equipment. Four sticks—two sticks 1/2 inch in diameter and two 1/4 inch in diameter. The sticks may also be decorated or wrapped in buckskin thong within their pairs. You also need a blanket or mat for covering the sticks and some counters to keep score.

Playing the Klamath four-stick game (scoring has been simplified). There are six possible patterns of stick arrangement:

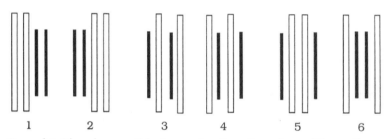

Round 1. The players sit facing each other. One player (Player A) arranges the four sticks under the blanket in any one of the patterns. His opponent (Player B) guesses which pattern he thinks is correct (from his perspective).

If B's guess is right:	If B's guess is wrong:
Player B collects two counters and takes the sticks, becoming Player A	Player A collects one counter and, keeping two sticks covered, arranges the other two so Player B can see them

Round 2. Player B guesses the pattern of four sticks again.

If B's guess is right:	If B's guess is wrong:
Player B collects one counter and takes the sticks, becoming Player A	The game proceeds as in Round 1

The game ends when one player has acquired all the counters.

CHIPPEWA MOCCASIN GAME

Object of the game. To hide or locate a small object in one of four containers.

Number of players. Two.

Equipment. Four small objects, one marked to distinguish it from the other three, and four containers or cloth pads ("moccasins") to conceal the objects. Twenty counting sticks for each player and a couple of long sticks for striking or turning the moccasins are also needed.

Playing the moccasin game. A blanket is laid out and players sit on it facing each other. Counting sticks are divided equally between the players. A knife is thrown in the air; when it lands on the blanket, the person its blade points to becomes the first player to hide the objects. He holds the objects in one hand and picks up the end of each container, one at a time, with the other hand. As he does so, and swaying and moving to the drum beat, he deposits one object under each container.

His opponent uses a striking stick to turn over the moccasin he thinks conceals the marked object. He must be careful, however! Only the third guess gains him points. If he displays the odd object on the first guess, he loses four sticks; on the second, he loses three sticks. Displaying the odd object on the third guess gains him four sticks from his opponent. If the object is *not* discovered on the third guess, he loses four sticks.

The winner is the player who collects all the counting sticks.

WALAPAI HIDDEN-BALL GAME

This is a very boisterous game and a game of great fun for players and spectators alike. Bystanders and team members often rush in and attempt to influence (rightly or wrongly!) the choices of the players.

Object of the game. To hide or locate a ball hidden in a pile of sand.

Number of players. Any number in two teams, but only one from each team participates in any given round.

Equipment. Sixteen counting sticks (Spanish bayonet stems in the southwest) and a small ball. In an area with soft dirt or sand, two trenches are dug parallel to each other; their dimensions should be 3-4 feet long, 6-8 inches deep, and 12 inches wide. The loose dirt is left in the trenches and the counting sticks are placed on the ground between them.

Playing the hidden ball game. One player takes the ball in his left hand and buries his hand at one end of the trench. Continuing to pile sand over his hand, he gradually draws his hand to the other end of the trench. He withdraws his hand empty, having left the ball somewhere in the loose dirt. He then divides the earth in the ditch into four piles by piling it up with his hands.

An opponent now runs his hands into one of the piles. If he finds the ball, the ball changes sides and the finder hides it in his own trench. If he does not find it, the hider has the option to allow him a second chance before a miss is scored. When a miss is determined, the hider takes a counter from the pile and hides the ball a second time.

The game continues until the center pile of counters is in the possession of the two players (or teams). Then when a player misses, the hider takes his counter from his opponent's cache. The game is won when all the counters are one side.

GAMES OF DEXTERITY

Indian dexterity games focused on tests of hunting skill, strength, and agility. Culin divides those games into five types: archery and arrow games, games that involved sliding a lance or arrow across hard ground or ice, shooting or throwing darts or lances at a moving ring, ball games in highly specialized forms, and racing games (which were often interrelated with ball games).

Archery games. Archery games were played with arrows, darts, and similar objects that were shot or tossed at a mark. Two examples (Pawnee, Pima) are included here.

Snow snake games. Snow snake games were confined to northern tribes who lived where snow and ice were abundant during part of the year. Though basically men's games, special forms did exist for women.

There are three distinct variations of snow snake. The first consists of a long polished rod that is made to glide over the frozen surface (the example is the Arapaho snow snake). The second type is a bone slider decorated with two feathers (Cheyenne snow slider). The third is a javelin or ski-like dart which skims along the ground or through the air, often after being launched by a raised bump of ice or earth (snow darts).

Hoop-and-pole games. Hoop-and-pole games were played throughout the United States and Canada. There was wide diversity, both in the equipment used and in the method of play. The hoop (target) could be a simple circle or a hoop that was intricately netted, beaded, feathered, and colored. The pole could be an arrow (shot or thrown), a lance, or a dart.

Gambling on the outcome was a favorite pastime. Three variations are offered here—a very simple hoop-and-pole game, the disc and cross game, and a target-and-pin game.

Ball and racket games. Many ball games were rough and dangerous to the players. This book describes two of the most popular—shinny and early lacrosse.

Ball races. The last type of game appears to have been most popular in the southwestern United States and Mexico. Ball races were early games—their existence has been documented in cliff dwellings. Sometimes they were run as intertribal competitions and betting was popular. As with dice games, balls often had ceremonial significance. For example, the Hopi buried kicking cylinders in springs and shrines. The Acoma, who played from March to May to ask for rain, buried their kicking sticks in their cornfields.

"Balls" were as diverse as stone or wood balls, rings, animal bladders, lumps of hair stuck together with piñon gum, and sticks. The size of the balls also varied; a few were relatively large, but most were about 2 to 3 inches in diameter. Players ran individually or in teams, most often over a predetermined course. Use of hands and fingers was not allowed.

PAWNEE ARROW GAME

Object of the game. To throw two arrows and stick them in the ground, the second going farther than the first.

Number of players. Any reasonable number.

Equipment. Two arrows for each player.

Playing the Pawnee arrow game. Each player takes an arrow between his thumb and index finger. He throws it, attempting to stick it in the ground twenty or thirty paces in front of him. He takes a second arrow and, stepping forward, attempts to stick the second arrow 4-5 feet beyond the first. Any arrow that fails to stick fast in the ground is forfeited.

PIMA ARROW GAME

Object of the game. To stick an arrow in a moving bundle of rags.

Number of players. Any number of men.

Equipment. Two arrows for each player—one deposited in a pile, the other held in hand—and a bundle of rags on a string.

Playing the Pima arrow game. The players, each holding one arrow, stand in a circle. One boy is chosen to run around the outside of the circle dragging the string with the bundle of rags. The player who can throw his arrow and sink it into the rags wins the pile of arrows. The runner is paid a few arrows for his effort.

ARAPAHO SNOW SNAKE

Object of the game. To hurl the snake so that it goes farther through the air and along the snow than any competitor's snake.

Number of players. Commonly two girls played against each other. The game is easily adapted to more than two and could be played by children and adults of both sexes.

Equipment. Slender willow rods about 4 feet long that have been peeled and painted and tipped with a buffalo horn point to make them slide easily.

Playing Arapaho snow snake. Each competitor holds the rod between her thumb and finger, pointing forward, with her arm at her side. To release the snake, she swings her arm back and forth and releases the rod forward. The winner is the owner of the rod that goes the farthest.

CHEYENNE SNOW SLIDERS

Object of the game. To make the slider go the farthest from a starting line.

Number of players. Any number.

Equipment. Simple sliders can be made from beef or pork rib bones. Clean them well, smooth them, and drill two holes in one end of each bone. Glue in two feathers (size and configuration are up to you—experiment to see what works best). You may decorate the bones with drilled patterns or paint. Finally, varnish the bones to give them a glossy surface.

Playing Cheyenne snow sliders. The slider is placed with the convex side down. The player places his thumb on one side of the bone, his middle, ring, and little fingers on the other side; the index finger is bent and placed against the end of the bone with the feathers. The player throws the slider down and forward against ice, pushing it out with the index finger, so it moves forward. The winner is the person who slides his slider the longest distance from a given starting line.

SNOW DARTS

Object of the game. To skim the dart along the ice for a longer distance than those of opponents.

Number of players. Any number.

Equipment. Chippewa snow darts varied in length, most being from 12 inches to about 30 inches. The Menominee darts were sometimes as long as 6 feet. Darts were often decorated with faces to represent snakes. Some possible styles and lengths are shown below:

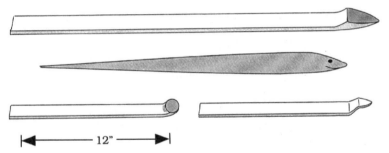

|◄——————— 12" ———————►|

Playing snow darts: The player stands at right angles to the direction his snake will travel. He places his hand or index finger at the end of the tail. Stooping over and holding the snake horizontally, he pushes the head forward, causing it to skim along the ice. The Chippewa often built a ridge of snow sloping away from the players, so the snake would become airborne and sail through the air for part of its distance.

HOOP-AND-POLE GAME

Hoop-and-pole games were played exclusively by males, often by only two players. The outcome could be determined in complex ways, depending on the tribe and on how the poles fell in reference to the inside of the hoop. A very simple version is presented here.

Object of the game. To stop the hoop from rolling by throwing the pole through it as it rolls.

Number of players. Any number

Equipment. Each player needs a lance or a dart to throw. Darts are easier for small children and can be made from a straight sapling about 3 feet long. When it has been smoothed and sharpened, the dart can be personalized and decorated with a variety of materials, such as paint, cloth, beads, and feathers.

Hoops can be almost any size; the most common today have a diameter of 14 to 36 inches (the smaller the hoop, the more difficult it is to throw a pole through it). To make a hoop, you can bend willows or saplings into a circle.

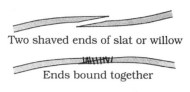

The ends can be shaved to a smooth, tapered edge and overlapped, then bound together with rawhide.

If you want a webbed hoop, rawhide makes good webbing and can be woven in a variety of patterns. Tie or overlap an end to anchor it, then weave the rawhide over and under as your pattern develops. Tie the rawhide to the rim with a lark's head knot.

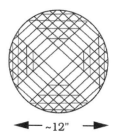

Possible
webbing pattern

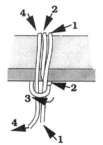

Lark's head knot to tie
webbing to rim

If you need longer rawhide as you weave, splice it like this:

Playing hoop and pole. Holding their darts or lances, players line up in one line about 20 feet from the path of the rolling hoop (or two parallel lines, each about 20 feet on either side of the path of the hoop). A non-player rolls the hoop rapidly along the ground in front of the players' line (or midway between the players' lines). Each player throws his pole at it, trying to stop the hoop by sticking his pole through it into the ground. When the hoop stops, the shaft must be within the rim or the shot does not count.

Scoring may be kept in any way that is agreeable to the players. Some tally the number of successes each player has over a given number of hoop rolls; the player with the greatest number wins. Others require that the players drop out as they miss the hoop; the winner is the player left at the end.

DISC AND CROSS

Disc and cross is one of the few games believed to be borrowed from Europeans. Though the game originated in France and was very popular during the reign (1830-1848) of Louis-Philippe of Orleans, early colonists brought the game to the New World much before the nineteenth century.

Object of the game. To hit the opponents' rolling disc with another disc.

Number of players. Four as two competing couples (X and Y below).

Equipment. Two 12-inch discs, which can be either solid pieces of wood or hoops painted two distinct colors, and four brightly colored posts, sharpened on one end. Good posts can be made by cutting two broom handles in half and adding a wooden ball to the top of each one.

Playing disc and cross. The game is played on a flat dirt surface or grass. The posts are stuck in the ground in a square, the dimensions of which can be agreed upon by the players.

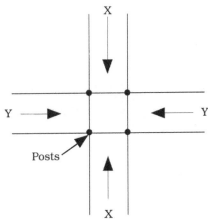

One couple (X) rolls their disc back and forth between them. The other couple (Y) tries to roll theirs so it hits X's disc in the square formed by the posts. When a roll makes a successful hit, 1 point is scored and the couples reverse their roles. Play continues until one couple accumulates an agreed-upon number of points. Then the area of the target square is reduced by moving the posts in and players begin again.

TARGET-AND-PIN GAMES

Target-and-pin games are analagous to the European "cup and ball" game, in which a ball on a string is tossed in the air and caught in a small cup. It is also a kind of solitaire hoop-and-pole game. The Native Americans used a number of materials as the object to be caught: rings, pharyngeal bones, skulls of small rodents, webbed hoops, glass beads, twig or animal-hair bundles, and (commonly) a flap of buckskin with holes in it. The pin was originally a wood or bone needle, but wire can be used.

Object of the game. To impale an object on a pin. Children play target-and-pin for their own amusement. The Penobscot used a moose-hair bundle to determine if a young man's courting was acceptable to a young woman.

Number of players. One (opposing players can play for wagers).

Equipment. The materials and construction of target-and-pin games can be made of many different things. A few examples are given below to give you some ideas of what you might use to construct a game. Use your imagination!

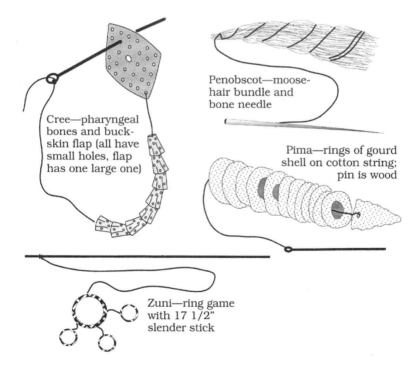

Cree—pharyngeal bones and buckskin flap (all have small holes, flap has one large one)

Penobscot—moose-hair bundle and bone needle

Pima—rings of gourd shell on cotton string; pin is wood

Zuni—ring game with 17 1/2" slender stick

Playing a target-and-pin game. The object of the game is to hold the pin in your hand and sling the object forward and up in an arc, catching it on the point of the pin. Points and winners can be determined as you decide; in part this will be regulated by the materials of your game, the number and size of the holes, and other considerations.

SHINNY

Shinny is a ball game that was almost universal among the North American tribes. It was often considered a women's game, though men also played. In some tribes, the sexes joined together; in others, they played separately. In the Crow tribe, men competed against women. The game had few rules except that the ball could never be touched with the hands. Shinny could be a brutal game that resulted in many injuries.

Object of the game. To bat a ball across the opponents' goal.

Number of players. Two teams—the more, the merrier!

Equipment. A small ball from 3 1/2 to 4 inches in diameter; originally balls were made of wood (often a knot) or buffalo hair covered with buckskin. Each player also has a stick about 39 inches long and curved at one end, similar to today's hockey stick.

Playing shinny. Two goals are set at opposite ends of a field. These may be identified by posts, a tree, a line. Depending on local custom, goals could be any distance apart from 220 yards to 1,400 yards. To start the game, the ball is thrown in the air in the center of the playing area. By hitting the ball with their sticks (some games allowed kicking), each team tries to force the ball past the other team's goal.

LACROSSE

The formal lacrosse game we know today is quite different from the rough game played by the Native Americans. Many tribes had ball-and-racket games, but they were less widely distributed than shinny. For example, racket games are unrecorded in the southwestern United States. Success was very important—racket and ball games were a kind of ritualized warfare and winners gained prestige. Because numerous wagers were made, winning also brought economic gain. To ensure success, dances, taboos, and other rituals and mystic rites—some quite bloody—came to be part of the preparation.

Lacrosse was not always played year-round. Some groups, such as the Winnebago, played lacrosse most often at a spring rendezvous with trappers after the winter hunt; they seldom played at other times in their villages.

Object of the game. To carry a ball with a racket and toss it against the goalpost of the opponents.

Number of players. Lacrosse was a man's game and great numbers, divided into two teams, participated.

Equipment. Originally balls were probably made of wood, but later ones were constructed from deerskin stuffed with hair and flattened into a thick round disc. The diameters of balls varied; the most popular seemed to be between 2 1/4 inches and 3 inches.

Each player also needs a racket. Rackets varied in length and shape, depending on the tribe. You can make either of two simple ones from willow:

Cut a withe that is about 5 feet long and 1 5/8 inches in diameter at the base. Mark the withe about 20 inches down from the top (narrow) end.

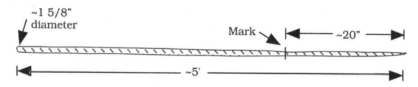

Pare one side of the withe from your mark to the narrow end, making the taper about half its original thickness. Pare carefully, taking off just enough to allow the pared portion to bend easily.

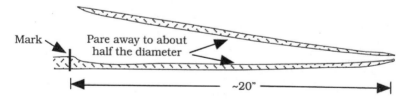

From this point, you have two choices for the type of racket you want. For the first, bend the pared end into an oval, overlapping it 4 inches along the handle behind the paring. Bind the overlap with leather or wet rawhide strips (rawhide works best) and tuck in the ends.

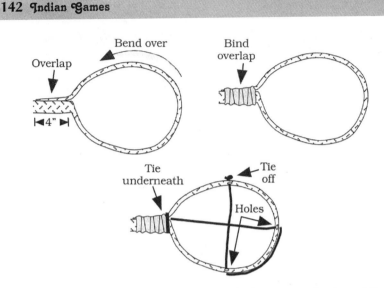

When the rawhide is dry, drill 3/16-inch holes, one at the top of the racket and two about halfway down the sides opposite each other. Tie a strip of leather thong underneath the racket at the top of the handle. Take it through the hole in the top, across the outside and into a side hole, then across to the opposite hole. Snug it up and tie it off.

For the second type of racket, bend the trimmed willow and overlap the end 6 inches to make a circle. Bind the overlap with wet rawhide, extending the binding down the shaft. To string the racket, drill eight holes evenly

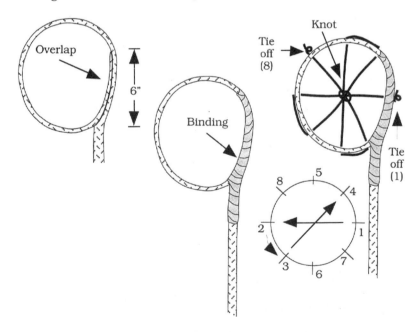

spaced around the circle. Begin stringing with a hole in the binding (#1 in diagram), tying off the end. Bring the thong through hole #1 and across the circle to the opposite hole (#2). Take the thong through the hole to the outside, across the outside of the circle to hole #3, to the inside through that hole, across to hole #4, and so on through hole #7. On the way to hole #8, tie all the thongs together with a snug knot centered in the willow loop. Then continue through hole #8 and tie off the thong.

Playing lacrosse. Two posts or goals are planted at a large distance apart, e.g., for the Ojibway, the posts were one-third of a mile apart! Players scatter themselves across the field. Often the best players are near the center of the playing area, the biggest between the center and their respective goals, and the poorest near the goal.

Play begins by someone tossing the ball into the air in the center of the field. As it comes down, the players try to capture it with their sticks. When one succeeds, he races toward his opponents' goal. If he is too closely pursued, he may choose to toss it to one of his teammates.

Opponents try to dislodge the ball by striking the handle of the ball stick. Often the ball carrier is injured by being hit on the arm or the leg. If the ball becomes free, the opposition players try to take it up and reverse direction to *their* opponents' goal. And, of course, the team that has the ball tries to retrieve it and continue forward.

When the ball carrier reaches his destination goal, he must throw the ball so it touches the post. The opposition players guarding the post may deflect the ball or catch it in their rackets and throw it back into the field.

The winning side can be the one that has the greatest number of scores when both teams decide to quit. As with shinny, the fervor which characterizes a lacrosse game makes it very dangerous indeed.

MOHAVE BALL RACE

Object of the game. To be the first racer to run, kicking a ball, around a course and back to the starting point.

Number of players. Two (other tribes sometimes had teams of several racers who ran in a relay). In the Mohave game, each racer had a second who ran behind him during the run.

Equipment. A ball about 2 inches in diameter for each racer (or team). The Mohave ball was made of mesquite wood.

Ball racing. A goal, one or two miles distant, is agreed upon. A line is drawn at the starting point and each racer places his ball on it, separating the balls by 5 or 6 feet.

The racers drop back about 10 feet behind the line. At a signal from the seconds, each racer rushes to his ball, pushes his foot under it, and tosses it forward as far as he can. Continuing the same way, he moves the ball toward the goal, where he reverses direction and comes back to the starting point.

The winner is the first player to put his ball over the starting line. He collects any bets made on the outcome.

SUPPLIERS

GAME EQUIPMENT

Old-time game equipment, such as English and American playing cards, wooden dice and dominoes, clay marbles, jackstraws, tops, cup-and-ball games, tavern puzzles, and some game boards are available from a number of sources, including:

Ray Glazner
Images of the Past
903 Parcher St. West
Wausau, WI 54403
(715) 849-1840
FAX: (715) 849-2840

Smoke and Fire Trading Co.
PO Box 166
Grand Rapids, OH 43522
(419) 832-0303
FAX: (419) 832-5008

An elaborate paper copy of the game of goose board is printed at Colonial Williamsburg and can be purchased from:

Colonial Williamsburg
Visitor Center Gift Shop
102 Visitor Center Drive
Williamsburg, VA 23185
Phone: (757) 229-1000

INDIAN DICE

A set of four Tarahumara stick dice (item number XM10) for a game called romavoa (quince in Spanish) is available from:

Native Seed/SEARCH
526 N. 4th Ave.
Tucson, AZ 85705
Phone: (520) 622-5561
FAX: (520) 268-9233

BIBLIOGRAPHY

A delightful book about some remarkable gamblers is:

Hutchens, J.K., ed. *The Gambler's Bedside Book.* New York: Taplinger Publishing Co., Inc., 1977.

Your local library has a number of good game books, including those that describe games played for a long time. Much of the information for the games in this book came from:

Arnold, P., ed. *The Book of Games.* New York: Exeter Books, 1985.

Arnold, P. *The Encyclopedia of Gambling.* Secaucus, NJ: Chartwell Books, Inc., 1977.

Botermans, J., T. Burrett, P. van Delft, and C. van Splunteren. *The World of Games.* New York: Facts on File, Inc., 1989.

Culin, S. *Games of the North American Indians.* New York: Dover Publications, Inc., 1975.

Encyclopedia Britannica, 15th ed., s.v. "hazard."

Gilgun, B. 1999. Tidings from the 18th Century (Some Diversions at the Games Table). *Muzzleloader,* March/April, 23-28.

Goodfellow, C. *A Collector's Guide to Games and Puzzles.* Secaucus, NJ: Chartwell Books, 1991.

Grunfeld, F.V., ed. *Games of the World.* New York: Holt, Rinehart and Winston, 1975.

Hoyle, E. *The Official Rules of Card Games: Hoyle up to Date, 1887.* Cincinnati: United States Card Company, 1940.

Kalman, B. *Games From Long Ago.* New York: Crabtree Publishing Co., 1995.

Kalter, J. *String Figures.* New York: Drake Publishers, Inc., 1978.

Levine, S. and V. Scudamore. *Marbles: A Player's Guide.* New York: Sterling Publishing Co., Inc., 1998.

Morehead, A.H. *The Official Rules of Card Games–Hoyle Up to Date.* Cincinnati, OH: The United States Playing Card Company, 1959.

Morehead, A.H., R.L. Frey, and G. Mott-Smith. *The New Complete Hoyle Revised.* New York: Doubleday, 1991.

Provenzo, A.B. and E.F. Provenzo, Jr., *Play It Again.* Englewood Cliffs, NJ: Prentice-Hall, Inc., 1981.

Riley, G. and R.W. Etulain, eds. *By Grit and Grace.* Golden, CO: Fulcrum Publishing, 1997.

Smith, B.C. *After the Revolution.* New York: Random House, Inc., 1985.

Tilley, R. *Playing Cards.* London: Octopus Books, Ltd., 1973.

Vecchione, G. *The World's Best Street & Yard Games.* New York: Sterling Publishing Co., Inc., 1989.

Wood, C. and G. Goddard. *The Complete Book of Games.* New York: Blue Ribbon Books, Inc., 1938.

INDEX